ILLUSTRATORS SOURCEBOOK

1850 TO THE PRESENT DAY

NICK & TESSA SOUTER

FOREWORD
BY
PAUL HOGARTH

PICTURE RESEARCH
BY
ANNE MARIE EHRLICH

Macdonald Orbis

A *Macdonald Orbis* Book

Copyright © 1990
Quarto Publishing plc.

First published in Great
Britain in 1990 by
Macdonald & Co
(Publishers) Ltd London
and Sydney.
A member of Maxwell
Pergamon Publishing
Corporation plc.

ISBN 0 356 17842 0

This book was designed
and produced by Quarto
Publishing plc,
The Old Brewery,
6 Blundell Street,
London,
N7 9BH.

Project Director
Moira Clinch
Editors
Kate Kirby
Angie Gair
Designers
Hugh Schermuly
Karin Skånberg
Penny Dawes
David Kemp
Picture Researcher
Anne Marie Ehrlich
Art Director
Nick Buzzard
Editorial Director
Carolyn King

Typeset by
Burbeck Associates,
Harlow
Manufactured in Hong
Kong by Regent Publishing
Services Ltd.
Printed by Leefung-Asco
Printers Ltd, Hong Kong.

Macdonald & Co
(Publishers) Ltd,
Orbit House,
1 New Fetter Lane,
London EC4A 1AR.

Special thanks to
Michael Felmingham,
David King, Mark Hames
of Forbidden Planet, Stuart
Newman, Eileen Evans.

ILLUSTRATION HAS LONG SUFFERED at the hands of even the most well-informed art critic. "Mere illustration"—the most common derogatory remark levelled at paintings that have sought to express or convey an idea—says it all. The cliché is both absurd and meaningless, especially today, when many artists refuse to recognize the artificial barrier between commercial and fine art. Moreover, it does not necessarily follow that an artist working to a brief is little more than a hack. Granted, some are, but the professional illustrator is the modern counterpart of the Renaissance painter, an artist who will frequently transcend the most mundane of briefs to provide the mass audience with Art.

The *Illustrator's Souce Book* is a hugely diverse gallery of graphic art created by the world's leading illustrators and proves my case beyond doubt. Here are assembled artists of the book and the magazine, designers of posters, reporters and satirists of the social scene, travellers and painter-illustrators. Popular artists as well as more significant artists, minor figures as well as great ones. In short, the whole spectrum of image-making that comprises the art of illustration.

We are first introduced to the illustrators of the 19th century, artists active between 1850 and 1900. Their work appeared in books and magazines aimed at a buoyantly literate middle-class public, to whom reading had become as much a habit as watching television is to us today. For almost an entire century these artists were at the mercy of the engraver. Until the late 1870s, Victorian printing technology was compelled to rely on wood-engraving as the sole means of reproducing an artist's design. It was a laborious process which usually obliterated the spontaneity of an original, although occasionally it could produce surprises. Only if the artist was familiar with the practice of drawing *directly* onto the woodblock with brush or pen and black ink could idiosyncrasies of style survive. Adolf Von Menzel in Germany, Charles Keene and Houghton in Britain, were foremost among those who learnt from Hokusai and other masters of the *Ukiyo-e.* Guided by enlightened master engravers like the Brothers Dalziel, Joseph Swain and William Luson Thomas, they succeeded in overcoming the daunting limitations of the medium.

As the 19th century drew to an end, photomechanical technology came to the rescue, making possible a breakthrough in both colour printing and in reproduction of black-and-white originals. This was the decade of Aubrey Beardsley and Phil May, of Charles Dana Gibson and Howard Pyle, of E J Sullivan and Paul Renouard. At this time also, the painter's contribution to illustration grew rapidly, now that it had become possible to reproduce drawings with great fidelity. One of the pleasures of looking through Parisian weeklies of the era, such as *L'Assiette au Beurre* and *Le Rire*, is in discovering editorial drawings by Juan Gris, Eugène Higgins, Frantisek Kupka, Lautrec, Jacques Villon and Kees Van Dongen, not forgetting the dramatic input of Käthe Kollwitz, Alfred Kubin and Jules Pascin in the pages of the Munich weekly, *Simplicissimus*.

Good illustration, of course, knows no frontiers. If at one period the ball is not to be found in the court of the British or the Americans, it will be found in the court of the French or the Germans. One thinks of the revival of lithography which led to the golden era of the poster in *belle époque* France. One thinks also of the Berlin of the 1920s and of the extraordinary satirical journalism in which a brilliant generation of editors, poets and essayists made common cause with artists like George Grosz, Otto Dix and John Heartfield, to castigate what they felt to be an unjust system.

Indeed, the ball goes back and forth constantly. One is also reminded of American illustration of this time; the advent of superb story illustration in the *Saturday Evening Post* and *Collier's*, a reportorial tradition which lasted through World War II and into the 1960s in *Fortune, Sports Illustrated* and *Rolling Stone*. In fact, American illustration flourishes right up to the present day in a host of new periodicals which also publish a younger generation of European illustrators, thus ensuring the cross-fertilization that is such a vital part of illustration.

William Morris maintained that illustration, though not vital to people's existence, nonetheless gave a great deal of aesthetic pleasure and was therefore a subject worthy of attention and encouragement. The *Illustrator's Source Book* confirms this to be true in no uncertain terms.

Paul Hogarth

BEFORE ASSESSING THE ROLE of the illustrator within society it is perhaps appropriate to consider first his or her position in the world of art.

For many years the notion has prevailed that, in the company of fine artists, the illustrator is something of a second-class citizen. This discrimination is predicated on the belief that the painter or sculptor is an unfettered spirit whose work gives free reign to self expression and whose art makes statements of an intensely personal nature. Illustrators, on the other hand, are the slaves of commerce—they are invariably commissioned to produce their work, and their inspiration derives, not from personal experience, but from the source material with which they are provided.

Under scrutiny, this delineation quickly blurs. Some of the world's greatest art treasures were in fact commissioned, whether by the Church, the State or by private individuals. For example, Michelangelo's paintings in the Sistine Chapel, while infused with an intensely personal vision, were nonetheless inspired by the writings of that all-time best seller, the Bible.

The fact is that all artists, whether painters, sculptors or illustrators, face very much the same predicament: they all work within constraints from which only the power of their imagination can free them. With the skills and materials available to them, they endeavour to create a unique interpretation of an idea, event or observation, and it is this shared aim that validates the role of illustrator within the world of the arts.

Historically, there have been differing schools of thought on the role of illustration. At one extreme we have Eric Gill, who believed that illustration should "really illustrate, clarify and illuminate the text" and not be used for "outpourings of sensibility". At the other extreme, we find the German Expressionist illustrators, such as Lovis Corinth, whose drawings were seldom literal and who often subordinated the illustration of the text to the expression of the artist's state of mind. And quite outside of this spectrum there was the Edwardian passion for gift books, which merely served as vehicles for the artists' explorations of their illustrative, imaginative and decorative skills. However, irrespective of the style adopted and the subject matter chosen, the illustrator performs simultaneously, and sometimes unwittingly, in a secondary role—that of social historian.

Our view of history would be somewhat myopic were it not illuminated by such a wealth of illustrations for both fictional and documentary material. In Britain, artists such as John Everett Millais and Fred Walker meticulously recorded the details of Victorian life in illustrations for contemporary novels by Trollope and Thackeray. Less inadvertent were the commentaries on the state of the nation by Frank Holl and Luke Fildes, who set out to expose the poverty of urban life, or the scathing satires of monarchy, society and politics by Gillray, Rowlandson and Cruickshank. Even the 1890s passion for nostalgic and idealized depictions of country life informs us of a yearning for a pre-industrial world. In fact there is very little in the way of human behaviour and feeling that has escaped the conscious investigation or unconscious recording of the illustrator.

Another role, now mostly usurped by the camera, is that of the illustrator as journalist. With the development of the newspaper in the middle of the 18th century there was an increasing demand for the pictorial coverage of topical events. In 1854 William Simpson was sent on assignment to the Crimea, and his drawings of the war mark the arrival of the "Special Artist", now more simply known as War Artist. The conditions and dangers of battle, combined with the urgency of the public's demand for the very latest information, meant that artists rarely had time to do more than sketch the situation, despatch the drawing and rely on the finishing artists at home to add the details. Yet, despite the aesthetic compromises that such disconnected teamwork entailed, the artist could still capture the spirit of the occasion.

Today, in matters of reportage, the camera reigns supreme over illustration for a public which prefers to construct its own interpretation of events seen, with apparent objectivity, through the eye of a lens. However, the tradition of the artist as reporter continues, and in many countries the courtroom remains an arena of human interest to which only the illustrator, and not the photographer, has access.

Of course, the involvement of the artist in current affairs is not limited to crime and war. A sphere of influence which remains as strong today as it ever did is caricature. While politicians and royalty may shield their eyes from the flash guns of the *paparazzi,* there is no escaping this cruelly exaggerated, yet precise, form of cartoon drawing. The word caricature is derived from the Italian *caricare,* which means "to overload", and it was in Italy during the mid to late 1500s that the artist Annibale Carracci discovered that if he deliberately overemphasized the characteristics of his friends he could "grasp the perfect deformity and thus reveal the very essence of a personality". During the 18th century this art form became popular with dilettantes and amateurs who had embarked upon the Grand Tour. But by the 1900s, when there was a fascination with the belief that physiognomy revealed a near-scientific insight into personality, caricature had fallen into the hands of serious political artists, who used it to pass judgement on topical events and lampoon the conceits of public figures.

There are few newspapers now in circulation that do not employ the talents of a caricaturist or political cartoonist. Depending on the editorial stance of the publication, these skills may be used simply to amuse the reader, or to seriously ridicule and possibly damage the credibility of the individuals depicted. It is this latter faculty that leads us to consider yet another role of the illustrator—that of propagandist.

Part of the psychosis of war involves the dehumanization of the opposing forces and, to this end, the art of the caricaturist can be used to supreme jingoistic effect. Since the development of newspapers and posters, there has not been a war effort or revolution that has not recruited ranks of illustrators to portray the enemy or oppressor as a gargoyle of iniquity. Some of the finest examples are to be found in the works of David Moor and Viktor Deni from the time of the Russian Revolution. Their vilification of the bourgeoisie as bloated, pig-like creatures could not have failed to focus the rage of the proletariat by reducing complex issues to simple, powerful symbols.

Although most extreme in times of conflict, the manipulative power of the illustrator has its place in peacetime, where it is used to great effect in the world of commerce and advertising. The same talents and techniques that can so successfully defame, can be just as effective in the process of idealization.

Advertising agencies did not start to appear in any great number until the 1920s, but the business itself dates back to the middle of the 19th century when, for the most part, it was in the hands of the manufacturers. For the first 50 years, in the absence of photography, the principal role of the artist was simply to draw an image of the product. But as competition increased it became necessary to create perceived differentials in virtually identical products, so as to legitimize superiority claims. This sleight of hand was accomplished by the illustrator, who created an image world into which the client's product could be placed in the most flattering light. A particularly good example is the sale in the late 1890s of Millais' painting *Bubbles* to the manufacturers of Pears' Soap. In its original form this sentimental depiction of a child blowing bubbles with soap suds would have evoked gentle feelings of innocence, the freshness of youth, beauty, protectiveness and warmth. With the addition of the Pears' logo at the top of the image, and a bar of Pears' soap near the feet of the child, many of these emotions would have been grafted onto the product, which could then be presented to the public as a safe, pure and wholesome way of cleansing the skin. Millais himself is said to have been outraged, but the campaign was enormously successful and nearly 100 years later it is possible to trace the imagery of Pears' advertising back to Millais' work.

As well as creating a suitable emotional and aesthetic context for a product, illustration also developed many of advertising's most effective selling tools—visual hyperboles for the exaggeration of quality, the animation of company logos for branding, the exploitation of the female form and, perhaps most important, the use of humour. The public may get tired of advertising but it never gets tired of laughing. And humour, exemplified by John Gilroy's cartoon advertisements for Guinness in the 1930s and 40s, can engage the attention and sympathy of even the most disaffected audience.

That humour should reach advertising via the illustrator is hardly surprising, since the role of entertainer is traditional to the artist. The cartoon strip, first developed by the German artist Wilhelm Busch in the mid-19th century, is now a feature of daily life—and since the early 1840s there has been a proliferation of magazines whose primary concern is to amuse.

Humour, however, plays little part in the last role that we should consider here, that of illustrator as teacher. This category needs to be broad enough to include the topographical work of such artists as A B Houghton, who visited the United States in 1870 and whose drawings helped to satisfy the craving for travel literature at that time. But it must also embrace the meticulous work of those technical illustrators who make the worlds of science, technology and nature comprehensible to us. Their skills face increasing competition from photography, which, along with complex computer graphics and digital technology, can now offer an illustrator's control over images that originated inside a camera. For some, that challenge will once again raise the illustrator-as-artist debate with the contention that the technical illustrator is no more than a copyist whose interpretive skills are put to little use. Be that as it may, the acknowledgement of those skills is important here, as without them we would have an incomplete picture of the multifarious roles that illustration plays in our world.

In putting together this book we have tried to cover the major twists and turns in illustration's developmental path since the middle of the 19th century. We have found that for much of this journey, illustrators have paid little heed to the direction of fine art and their progress cannot be described by a series of "isms" and schools of thought. However, many figures, such as Morris, Abbey, Pyle and Gill have exerted a lasting influence on the course that illustration is taking and we have tried to ensure that they are well represented.

Inevitably, due to the limitations of space and the scarcity of good material for reproduction, there are omissions and you may find that a favourite artist has not been included. For this we apologize, while hoping that, as a source book of styles, you will still find this volume to be compehensive and inspiring.

Our lasting impression as we come to the end of compiling these images is that at every point in its history illustration has been on the threshold of an exciting new development— and never more so than today. Technology and imagination, it would seem, know no bounds, and when one considers that illustrators can now generate original artwork on a Mackintosh computer, one can only wonder as to what the future may bring.

BY 1850 THE STAGE WAS SET for the dramatic entrance of the illustrator as the entertainer of the 19th century. In reaction to the bleakness of the Napoleonic war period, the previous years had seen a craving for culture spread across Europe. Literacy was increasing, and with the Victorian invention of the arm-chair and sofa, the first truly comfortable items of furniture, a new concept in urban recreation evolved: family get-togethers with reading material of one form or another providing the amusement.

At the same time the Industrial Revolution also provided the technology for mass marketing, and with the arrival of metal printing plates and chromolithography, publishers were in a position to satisfy the public's thirst for entertainment and knowledge. Their industry was transformed beyond recognition.

In mid-century France the relaxing of censorship laws, coupled with the artistic freedom afforded by the autographic litho process, encouraged a flourishing tradition of cari-cature. Surprisingly, in Britain it had the opposite effect: caricaturists who had achieved prominence in such magazines as *Punch* found that the litho stone softened their work, which then lacked the spiteful line more easily achieved on copper plate.

During these years London artistic life exerted a huge influence throughout the world of illustrators. The political upheavals on the Continent had led many disaffected artists to Britain, and their influence was in part responsible for the development of social realism between 1850 and 1890. The illustrations of the lives of the poor by artists such as Luke Fildes and Frank Holl were then exported to the world at large through the distribution of such magazines as *The Graphic* and the *Illustrated London News,* which were eagerly read by artists in America and on the Continent.

As this frenzy of illustrative activity continued, various schools of thought began to emerge from the community of artists and critics. In 1848 John Everett Millais, William Holman Hunt and Dante Gabriel Rossetti formed the Pre-Raphaelite Brotherhood in an attempt to recreate the naivety and moral realism of early Renaissance painting. With their strong literary leanings they are accredited by many with giving illustration the status of art and encouraging the practice of putting artists' names on the covers of books.

The 1860s are sometimes described as the "golden age of Victorian illustration". There was a fashion for drawings of contemporary life in the novels of Dickens, Thackeray and Trol-lope, newsagents and bookstalls were appearing in every street and at every railway station, libraries were making their first appearance and taxes had been repealed on newspapers, making them more affordable. During this period specialist magazines were developed, and in 1860 *The Queen,* the first magazine aimed directly at women, appeared and was such a suc-cess that other publishers soon followed suit. Magazines were enjoying similar popularity on the other side of the Atlantic where, with the development of half-tone reproduction, the American public was eagerly reading *Harper's, Century* and *McClure's* and enjoying the work of Charles Marion Russell and Howard Pyle.

After a brief period of decline in the 1870s, the 1880s saw a resurgence of interest and activity in book production. This was due in part to the influence of William Morris, the leading figure in the Arts and Crafts Movement as well as the private press movement, which had an impact on both European and American publishing. Morris founded the Kelmscott Press in 1891 and, with his principal illustrator Edward Burne-Jones, revived the tradition of medieval craftmanship and the art of the woodcut and helped create what he referred to as the age of the "Book Beautiful".

The intensely art-conscious 1890s saw the emergence of the Aesthetic Movement, which followed the ethos of "art for art's sake" and which Morris despised. Its style of *fin de siècle* morbidity and eroticism was best captured by Aubrey Beardsley, whose drawings were particularly suited to the process reproduction of the day. The Aesthetes were championed by Oscar Wilde, and although his eventual disgrace brought the movement into disrepute, the contribution of such exponents as Walter Crane, Randolph Caldecott and Kate Greenaway was critical to the subsequent development of fantasy illustration.

But the new processes did not just revolutionize book production. In the hands of Jules Cheret (who pioneered many of the developments in chromolithographic poster printing), Toulouse-Lautrec and Alphonse Mucha, they led to another golden age, that of the poster. This medium, which was to become so important to the advertising industry in the next century, became one of the most popular art forms, with members of the public literally tearing posters from the hoardings and taking them home.

CHAPTER ONE

1850-1899

EDWIN AUSTIN ABBEY (1852–1911)

Born in Philadelphia, U.S.A. Worked in a wood engraving studio and studied art at evening classes at the Pennsylvania Academy of Fine Arts. In 1871 he moved to New York, where the influence of French and German black and white art was transforming pen drawing. He produced small black and white illustrations for Harpers and Brothers, then illustrated some of their more successful books, including Christmas Stories *by Charles Dickens (1875),* Selections from the Poetry of Robert Herrick *(1882) and Oliver Goldsmith's* She Stoops to Conquer *(1887). In 1878 he settled in England and became a prolific illustrator, specializing in costume and figure subjects. In contrast to the decorative convention of the period, his meticulous attention to detail — which extended to his making every effort to achieve historical accuracy — achieved a realism that influenced a whole generation of younger artists. He exhibited his first oil painting at the Royal Academy in 1890, and was elected Royal Academician in 1902.*

1, 2 *BOOK:*
SHE STOOPS TO CONQUER
by Oliver Goldsmith

DATE: c. 1887

3, 4 *BOOK:*
SCHOOL FOR SCANDAL
by Richard Sheridan

DATE: 1885

1

2

3

4

Mrs. G. H. Gilbert as "Mrs Candour" in The School for Scandal

CHARLES HENRY BENNETT
(1829–1867)

Apparently untrained, he contributed to The
Comic Times *and* Comic News *between
1855 and 1865, when he joined* Punch
*magazine. He illustrated several books,
including Bunyan's* Pilgrim's Progress
(1859), Nine Lives of a Cat *(1860),* Stories
Little Breeches Told *(1862) and* The
Fables of Aesop *(1857). He also illustrated
for a number of magazines, including* The
Illustrated Times, The Cornhill Magazine,
Every Boy's Magazine *and* Punch.

1–3 *BOOK:*
THE FABLES OF AESOP

DATE: 1857

1

2

3

18

SIR EDWARD COLEY BURNE-JONES (1833–1898)

*Born in Birmingham, UK. He was educated at
Oxford University, where he met William
Morris, with whom he toured Belgium and
the cathedrals of northern France instead of
completing his studies. On his return to
England he worked with Dante Gabriel
Rossetti on the Morte D'Arthur murals at the
Oxford Union in 1857–8 and was on the
fringes of the Pre-Raphaelite Brotherhood.
Known foremost as a painter, he also
illustrated a number of books, including
Archibald Maclaren's* The Fairy Family
(1857), Morris's The Earthly Paradise,
which was never completed,
The Works of Geoffrey Chaucer *(1896)
and Dalziel's* Bible Gallery *(1881). Between
1892 and 1898 he designed books for the
Kelmscott Press. He received an honorary
degree from Oxford in 1881, was made a
baronet in 1894 and in 1889 won the Cross of
the Legion of Honour at the Paris Exposition.*

1 *BOOK:* GOOD WORDS	
DATE: 1862	
2 *BOOK:* BIBLE GALLERY *by Dalziel*	
DATE: 1881	
3 *PAINTING:* "THE DEPTHS OF THE SEA"	
DATE: 1886	

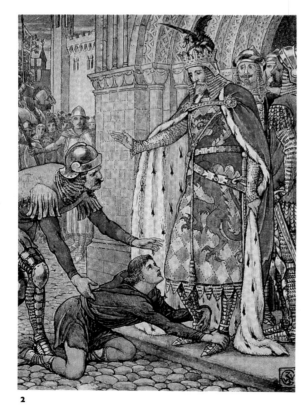

WALTER CRANE (1845–1915)

Born in Liverpool, UK. His illustrating career begun in 1863, when he was commissioned by Edmund Evans to illustrate three toy books for Warne publishers. Other books he illustrated include The House That Jack Built *(1865),* The Baby's Opera *(1877),* The Baby's Bouquet *(1878), Edmund Spenser's* The Faerie Queene *(published in 19 parts, 1894-97),* Ali Baba and the Forty Thieves *(1873) and* The Happy Prince and Other Stories *by Oscar Wilde (1888). Crane was also a painter, writer and designer of textiles, wallpapers and ceramics. His work was characterized by strong outlines, flat tints and solid blacks, and was influenced by his study of early printed books, medieval illuminations, Japanese prints and the work of the Pre-Raphaelites. He was converted to "conscious" socialism by William Morris and became a primary figure in the Arts and Crafts movement. In 1883 he joined the Socialist League and in 1884 was the first president of the Art Workers' Guild. He taught design at Manchester School of Art, was Art Director at Reading College and Principal of the Royal College of Art, 1898-99.*

1, 4 *BOOK:*
THE BLUEBEARD PICTURE BOOK

DATE: 1899

2 *BOOK:* ARTHURIAN LEGENDS

DATE: NOT KNOWN

3 *BOOK:* A FLOWER WEDDING

DATE: NOT KNOWN

5 *BOOK:*
A ROMANCE OF THE THREE Rs

DATE: 1886

6 *BOOK:* THE BABY'S BOUQUET

DATE: 1878

But in the meanwhile the Wolf went, with a grin,
    At the Grandmother's cottage to call;
He knocked at the door, and was told to come in,
    Then he eat her up—sad cannibal!
Then the Wolf shut the door, and got into bed,
    And waited for Red Riding Hood;
When he heard her soft tap at the front door, he said,
    Speaking softly as ever he could:

1

2

3

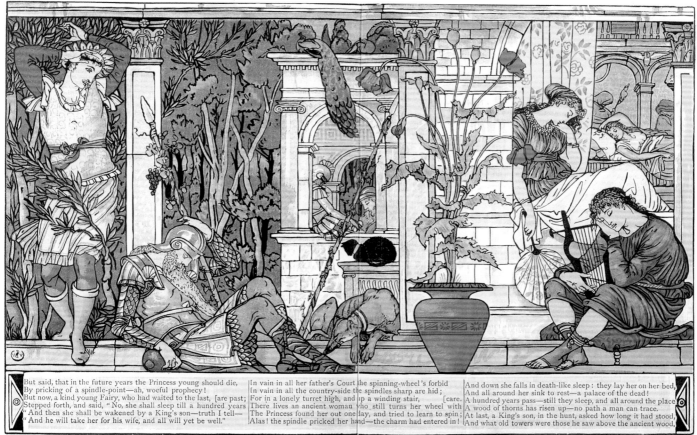

But said, that in the future years the Princess young should die,
By pricking of a spindle-point—ah, woeful prophecy!
But now, a kind young Fairy, who had waited to the last, [are past;
Stepped forth, and said, " No, she shall sleep till a hundred years
" And then she shall be wakened by a King's son—truth I tell—
" And he will take her for his wife, and all will yet be well."

In vain in all her father's Court the spinning-wheel 's forbid
In vain in all the country-side the spindles sharp are hid ;
For in a lonely turret high, and up a winding stair, [care.
There lives an ancient woman who still turns her wheel with
The Princess found her out one day, and tried to learn to spin ;
Alas ! the spindle pricked her hand—the charm had entered in !

And down she falls in death-like sleep : they lay her on her bed,
And all around her sink to rest—a palace of the dead !
A hundred years pass—still they sleep, and all around the place
A wood of thorns has risen up—no path a man can trace.
At last, a King's son, in the hunt, asked how long it had stood,
And what old towers were those he saw above the ancient wood.

4

5

6

WILHELM BUSCH (1832–1908)

Born in Hanover, Germany. Studied at academies in Dusseldorf, Antwerp and Munich. In 1859, his drawings began to appear in the leading comic weekly Fliegende Blatter, *but he soon moved from work for periodicals to self-contained albums of comic-strip narratives with verses accompanying the images. In this way he was able to develop the comic-strip form more fully and his work included social satire and cautionary tales. His best-known characters were the naughty children Max and Moritz, whose wicked pranks gave rein to Busch's talent for slapstick humour, but he was an innovative artist, producing graphic equivalents for emotional reactions and physical movement which subsequently became conventions of comic-strip art.*

1, 2 *BOOK:* BUZZ A BUZZ

DATE: 1872

3 *BOOK:* MAX UND MORITZ

DATE: 1871

RICHARD DADD (1817–1886)

Born in Kent, UK. He was educated at William Dadson's Academy of Art and the Royal Academy Schools in London, where he won the medal for life drawing in 1840. He contributed illustrations for The Book of British Ballads *(1842) and illustrated the frontispiece for* The Kentish Coronal *(1840). Dadd went insane while on a European tour with Sir Thomas Phillips, and was eventually committed to a mental asylum after he murdered his father in 1843. While in the asylum he was encouraged to continue painting, and produced works of incredible delicacy and beauty.*

1 *PAINTING:* THE FAIRY FELLER'S MASTER STROKE

DATE: 1864

1

"I'll get him up." A bee he took,
Impaled it on a fishing-hook;

Played it within his open jaws,
A bite! and up the frog he draws;

2

3

1

1

RICHARD DOYLE (1824–1883)

Born in London. He started drawing from a very early age and produced his first book, Home for the Holidays *(published in 1887), when he was only 12. His first published work, the comic medieval book* The Eglinton Tournament *(1840), was a great success. From 1843 he contributed regularly to* Punch, *and in January 1844 designed its sixth cover, a procession of figures based on Titian's* "Bacchus and Ariadne" *which remained unchanged until 1954. He eventually resigned from the magazine in protest against its anti-Catholic views and for the rest of his career concentrated on illustrating books. His own* Manners and Customs of Ye Englishe *(1849) and* Bird's Eye Views of Society *(1864) made him a household name. He also illustrated* The Fairy Ring *by the Brothers Grimm (1845), Mark Lemon's* The Enchanted Doll *(1849), Ruskin's* The King of the Golden River *(1851) and, his masterpiece, William Allingham's* In Fairyland *(1870), the illustrations for which were put to a new story in 1884,* The Princess Nobody *by Andrew Lang.*

1 *PAINTING:*
"THE KNIGHT AND THE SPECTRE"

DATE: NOT KNOWN

2 *BOOK:* THE PRINCESS NOBODY
by A D Lang

DATE: 1884

3, **4** *BOOK:* IN FAIRYLAND
by William Allingham

DATE: 1870

2

3

4

1

2

SIR LUKE FILDES (1844–1927)

*Born in Liverpool, UK. Studied at Warrington
School of Art and the South Kensington and
Royal Academy Schools in London. He was
renowned as a black and white artist in the
social realist vein, producing powerful images
of the poor and the destitute. Fildes' drawing of
Charles Dickens' study, entitled "The Empty
Chair", done the day after the author's death,
was published in* The Graphic *and was the
inspiration for van Gogh's painting "The
Yellow Chair". Fildes' illustrations also
appeared in* Sunday Magazine, The
Cornhill Magazine *and* The Gentleman's
Magazine. *He illustrated a number of books,
including Thackeray's* Catherine *(1894)
and Dickens'* Edward Drood *(1869). He
decided to concentrate on painting after 1872
and became a major portrait painter of the
Edwardian era. He was elected to the Royal
Academy in 1887 and was knighted in 1906.*

1 *MAGAZINE:*
SUNDAY MAGAZINE

DATE: 1866

2 *MAGAZINE:*
SUNDAY MAGAZINE

DATE: 1868

3 *MAGAZINE:*
SUNDAY MAGAZINE

DATE: 1868

3

ARTHUR HUGHES (1832–1915)

Born in London. He entered the Government School of Design at Somerset House at the unusually young age of 14, and at 15 enrolled at the Royal Academy Schools, where he won the silver medal for antique drawing two years later. In 1851 he first came into contact with the Pre-Raphaelite Brotherhood, and was subsequently involved in the painting of the Oxford Union murals with Dante Gabriel Rossetti and others. He also painted a number of famous pictures, including "Home from the Sea" *and* "The Long Engagement". *Hughes is best known for his black and white work and for his insistence on integrating his illustrations into the design of the book as a whole. His most notable period as an illustrator was his association with the writer George MacDonald, on books such as* At the Back of the North Wind *(1871),* The Princess and the Goblin *(1872) and* Phantasies *(1905). He also illustrated for magazines such as* The Graphic *and* Good Words for the Young.

I *PAINTING:*
"ALICE IN WONDERLAND"

DATE: NOT KNOWN

2,3 *MAGAZINE:*
GOOD WORDS FOR THE YOUNG

DATE: 1871

PAUL GUSTAVE CHRISTOPHE
DORE (1832–1883)

Born in Strasbourg. He learned lithography while still at school in Bourg-en-Bresse. At the age of 11 his family moved to Paris, where eventually he was placed under contract to Charles Philippon's Journal Pour Rire, *contributing a weekly page. He had his first lithographs published at the age of 13 and by the age of 22 he was already famous for his illustrated* Rabelais. *There followed a series of classic titles, including Dante's* Divine Comedy *(1861), Coleridge's* Rime of the Ancient Mariner *(1865), Tennyson's* The Story of King Arthur and Queen Guinevere *(1868) and Milton's* Paradise Lost *(1866). He also produced his own book of caricatures,* Two Hundred Sketches, Humorous and Grotesque *(1867). His work appeared in many publications, including* The Illustrated London News *and* The Illustrated Times.

1–4 *BOOK:* VISION OF HELL
by Dante

DATE: 1860

5 *BOOK:*
GARGANTUA ET PANTAGRUEL
by François Rabelais

DATE: NOT KNOWN

1

2

3

4

5

1

JOHN LEECH (1817–1864)

Born in London. Studied medicine at St Bartholomew's Hospital before deciding to become an artist. He soon made his name as a black and white artist, and illustrated for a number of periodicals, including The Sporting Review, Illustrated London Magazine, New Monthly Magazine *and* The London Magazine. *In 1840 he joined the staff of* Bentley's Miscellany, *and in 1841 he found a platform for his own brand of pictorial satire in the newly established journal* Punch. *But he was best known for his caricatures depicting Victorian middle-class life, epitomized in the characters of Tom Noddy and Mr Briggs. Books illustrated include* Etchings and Sketchings *(1835),* The Ingoldsby Legends *(1840),* Jack the Giant Killer *(1843) and* Uncle Tom's Cabin *(1852).*

| 1 *BOOK:* ASK MAMMA |
| *by R S Surtees* |
| *DATE:* 1858 |

| 2 *MAGAZINE:* PUNCH |
| *DATE:* 1881 |

2

"BUBBLES."
By Sir John Millais, Bt., P.R.A.
After the Original in the possession of Messrs. Pears

1

2

3

SIR JOHN EVERETT MILLAIS
(1829–1896)

Born in Southampton, UK. Studied at the Royal Academy Schools. In 1848 he founded the Pre-Raphaelite Brotherhood with Dante Gabriel Rossetti and Holman Hunt. He was much admired for his brilliant black-and-white illustrations, which, like those of the American Edwin Austin Abbey, show an incredible attention to detail and a concern for realism, both visual and moral. He illustrated the novels of Anthony Trollope, which were serialized in The Cornhill Magazine *in 1860, and contributed to* Punch *and the Pre-Raphaelite magazine* The Germ. *His best period is considered to have ended by 1863, when he was elected Royal Academician, by which time he had given up illustrating in favour of painting portraits and landscapes. In 1885 he was made a baronet and in 1896 became President of the Royal Academy, which he remained until his death from throat cancer six months later.*

1 *ADVERTISEMENT:*
PEARS SOAP
*(based on the original painting,
"Bubbles")*

DATE: 1886

2, 3 *BOOK:* THE DALZIEL BIBLE

DATE: 1864

GEORGE DU MAURIER (1834–1896)

*English, but born in Paris, the son of a
frustrated opera singer. He moved to London
as a child, and showed an early talent for
drawing. In 1851 he studied chemistry at
University College, London, but left in 1856 to
study art in Paris, where he met James
McNeill Whistler and E J Poynter. From
1857 to 1860 he studied in Antwerp under De
Keyser and Van Lerius, but the loss of an eye
forced him to abandon his plans to become a
painter and he returned to London to pursue a
career as a black and white artist. From 1860
he became a regular contributor to* Punch
*with his caricatures poking fun at the
Victorian bourgeoisie. He was the greatest
social satirist of the period, and the accuracy of
his ink drawings provides a complete chronicle
of Victorian life. He also illustrated for*
Harpers, The Graphic, The Illustrated
Times *and* The Cornhill *magazines, and in
middle age he wrote and illustrated three
novels,* Peter Ibbetson *(1891),* Trilby
(1894) and The Martian *(1896).*

1 BOOK: TRILBY *by George Du Maurier*	
DATE: 1894	
2 BOOK: OUR LIFE	
DATE: 1865	
3 MAGAZINE: CORNHILL MAGAZINE	
DATE: 1863	
4 BOOK: GOOD WORDS	
DATE: 1861	
5 BOOK: PICTURES OF ENGLISH LITERATURE	
DATE: 1870	
6 MAGAZINE: PUNCH	
DATE: c. 1860	

1

2

3

4

5

6

EDWARD LEAR (1812—1888)

Born in London. His unmarried sister Ann taught him to paint and, by the age of 15, he was already selling his drawings of birds. He made his name with his superb hand-coloured illustrations of parrots, published in 1832 as The Family of Psittacidae, or Parrots. *From 1832-36 Lear was employed by the Earl of Derby to draw his collection of rare birds and animals for a book, the privately printed* Knowsley Menagerie *(1856). For the amusement of the earl's children, he composed and illustrated humorous limericks in a deliberately childish, but wonderfully expressive style. These were published in 1846 as* A Book of Nonsense, *the popularity of which remained confined to upper-class households until a revised version of the book, published by Routledge-Warne in 1861, became a best-seller. His most famous rhymes,* Hey Diddle Diddle *and* The Owl and the Pussycat, *from* Nonsense Songs, Stories, Botany and Alphabets *(1871), are perennial favourites, probably more popular today than ever. His last book,* Laughable Lyrics, *was published in 1877.*

1, 2 *BOOK:* THE LEAR ALPHABET
by Edward Lear

DATE: 1871

3, 4 *BOOK:*
A BOOK OF NONSENSE
by Edward Lear

DATE: 1846

There was an Old Man of Marseilles, whose daughters wore bottle-green veils:
They caught several Fish, which they put in a dish,
And sent to their Pa at Marseilles.

There was an Old Man of Corfu, who never knew what he should do;
So he rushed up and down, till the sun made him brown,
That bewildered Old Man of Corfu.

ARTHUR BURDETT FROST
(1851—1928)

Born in Philadelphia, USA. At the age of 23 his first illustrated book, Out of the Hurly Burly, *sold over a million copies and launched his career. Frost was loved by Americans for his warm and humorous portrayal of animals and people. He was a master draughtsman and his drawings captured the mood and detail of rural American life. He had a remarkable sense of colour values, yet he was colourblind and his wife or sons had to label the colours of his palette for him. He illustrated the novels of Mark Twain, in which he created the enduring images of Tom Sawyer and Huckleberry Finn, but he is best known for his illustrations for Joel Chandler Harris's* Uncle Remus *and* Brer Rabbit *stories. In 1876 he joined the staff of* Harper's *and was cartoonist on the* New York Daily Graphic *for 20 years.*

1, 2 *BOOK:* UNCLE REMUS
by J Chandler Harris

DATE: 1893

3, 4 *BOOK:* A TANGLED TALE
by Lewis Carroll

DATE: 1886

1

2

ARTHUR BOYD HOUGHTON
(1836—1875)

Born in Kotagiri, Madras. Educated in England at Leigh's Academy and the Royal Academy Schools, where he came under the influence of the Pre-Raphaelite Brotherhood and developed an interest in Japanese prints — the effects of which are particularly evident in his illustrations for Dalziel's Arabian Nights *(1864). In 1869* The Graphic *magazine sent him on a journalistic assignment to the USA to draw the Americans and their way of life. The results are among his best work. His illustrated books include* Longfellow's Poems *(1867) and Dalziel's* Bible Gallery *(1880), and he contributed to* The Argosy, Every Boy's Magazine, The Sunday Magazine, The Graphic *and* The Broadway.

1, 2 *BOOK:* ARABIAN NIGHTS

DATE: 1864

3 *MAGAZINE:*
THE SUNDAY MAGAZINE

DATE: 1867

4 *MAGAZINE:*
THE SUNDAY MAGAZINE

DATE: 1867

3

4

1

2

3

SIR JOHN TENNIEL (1820–1914)

*Born in London. In spite of being accidentally
blinded in one eye during a fencing match with
his father, he was a superb draughtsman and
was essentially self-taught, having studied only
briefly at the Royal Academy Schools and the
Clipstone Street Life Academy. His
illustrations to* Aesop's Fables *(1848)
brought him to the attention of* Punch
*magazine, then at its most radical. He replaced
Doyle as a full-time member of staff in 1851,
and his pencil drawings over the next 50 years
summed up the essence of Victorian society. He
illustrated a number of books, but is best
known for his illustrations to the first edition of
Lewis Carroll's* Alice in Wonderland
*(1865). This was a difficult commission
because Carroll, disappointed at having his
own illustrations for the book rejected by the
publisher, consequently wanted complete
artistic control over Tenniel, which led to a
great many arguments. Because of these
difficulties, and in spite of the fact that* Alice
in Wonderland *achieved international
acclaim on publication, Tenniel initially
refused to illustrate the subsequent* Alice
Through the Looking Glass. *He finally
gave in, however, and it came out in 1871,
when it was an instant success. He was
knighted in 1893 and retired from* Punch
magazine at the age of 80.

1 *MAGAZINE:* PUNCH
DATE: 1853

2 *MAGAZINE:* PUNCH
DATE: 1853

3 *BOOK:* ALICE THROUGH THE LOOKING GLASS *by Lewis Carroll*
DATE: 1871

CECIL ALDIN (1870–1935)

Born in Slough, UK. Studied animal anatomy at the South Kensington School of Art, and animal painting under Frank W Calderon. Aldin's activities as a huntsman enabled him to draw the funny side of English country life, and his comic hunting scenes, olde worlde inns and dog-portraits, drawn in a jovial style, were immensely popular. He was particularly well known for his series of Puppy Dog *books (1904–14), which were favourites with children. Books include Hodder and Stoughton's* Christmas Eve *(1910), which owes much to the influence of Caldecott, and Anna Sewell's* Black Beauty *(1912). He contributed to numerous periodicals during the 1890s, including* The English Illustrated Magazine, Lady's Pictorial, Boy's Own Paper *and* Illustrated Sporting and Dramatic News.

1 *ADVERTISEMENT:* COLMAN'S BLUE

DATE: 1898

2 *ADVERTISEMENT:* COLMAN'S STARCH

DATE: c. 1898

3 *ADVERTISEMENT:* CADBURY'S COCOA

DATE: c. 1899

LOUIS RHEAD (1857–1926)

Born in Staffordshire, UK. Studied art in London and Paris, where meeting with Grasset proved a strong influence towards a career in poster design. He then emigrated to the USA, where he settled in Brooklyn. His work included portraits, posters and lithographs, ceramics, watercolour and line illustrations. Clients included The New York Sun, Scribner's *and* The Century. *Rhead's style owed much to Art Nouveau, but he was criticized for weak drawing, sometimes masked by over-elaboration of decorative elements. He collaborated with his brothers George and Frederick, individually and as a team, on book illustrations —* The Pilgrim's Progress *(1898), Tennyson's* Idylls of the King *(1898) and* Robinson Crusoe *(1900). He illustrated children's stories for* Harper's Bazaar, *and his own book as author and illustrator,* Bold Robin Hood and his Outlaw Band, *was published in 1923.*

1 *ADVERTISEMENT:* THE SUN MAGAZINE

DATE: 1894

2 *MAGAZINE COVER:* THE CENTURY

DATE: c. 1895

3 *MAGAZINE COVER:* SCRIBNER'S

DATE: c. 1895

4 *ADVERTISEMENT:* LUNDBORG PERFUME

DATE: c. 1895

THE LADY OF THE LAKE
TELLETH ARTHVR OF THE
SWORD EXCALIBVR

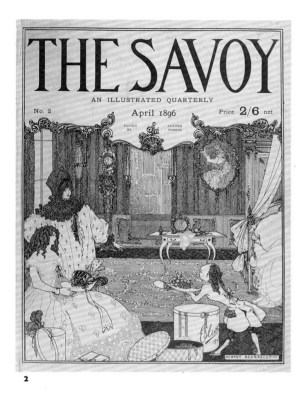

2

3

4

5

AUBREY VINCENT BEARDSLEY
(1872–1898)

Born in Brighton, UK. His family circumstances precluded any formal art training, though he had shown a talent for drawing and caricature while at school. While he was working as a clerk in London the artist Edward Burne-Jones encouraged him to attend evening classes at Westminster School of Art. In 1892 he visited Paris, where he was inspired by the posters of Toulouse-Lautrec and the current interest in Japanese prints. His first commission was from Messrs Dent, who asked him to illustrate their new edition of Malory's Le Morte d'Arthur *(1893). He then became Art Editor of* The Yellow Book *quarterly (1894–96) and illustrator for* The Savoy *(1896–98). Books illustrated include Pope's* The Rape of the Lock *(1896),* The Lysistrata of Aristophanes *(1896), Oscar Wilde's* Salomé *(1894) and* A Book of Fifty Drawings by Aubrey Beardsley *(1897). He developed his own highly personal version of the Art Nouveau style, featuring highly stylized forms, sinuous curves and the use of areas of heavy decoration set against areas of white space. His fascination with the decadence of the* fin-de-siècle *period was reflected in the sinister eroticism of his images, which shocked the public at the time. The acknowledged genius of black and white art, he influenced many subsequent artists. He died of tuberculosis at 25.*

I *BOOK:* LE MORTE D'ARTHUR
by Malory

DATE: 1893

2, 3 *MAGAZINE COVER:*
THE SAVOY

DATE: 1896

4, 5 *BOOK:* SALOME
by Oscar Wilde

DATE: 1894

RANDOLPH CALDECOTT
(1846–1886)

Born in Chester, UK. After leaving school he worked as a bank clerk while studying in the evenings at Manchester School of Art. There he met Thomas Armstrong, who showed Caldecott's work to the editor of London Society *magazine, who then published his first drawings in 1871. Caldecott's unfussy style, using strong outlines and flat areas of colour, was perfectly suited to children's book illustration and he was employed by the engraver Edmund Evans to take over the illustration of Routledge's* Shilling Toybooks *when his friend Walter Crane left after a quarrel about royalties. Caldecott had a particular love for the era that preceded the Industrial Revolution and his idealization of life in the country captured the hearts of the general public. Books illustrated include Washington Irving's* Old Christmas *(1875),* The Diverting History of John Gilpin, The House That Jack Built *(both 1878) and* Three Jovial Huntsmen Sing a Song of Sixpence *(1880). He also illustrated for* Punch, Boy's Own Paper *and* The Graphic.

1 *NURSERY POSTER*

DATE: 1884

2,3 *BOOK:*
RANDOLPH CALDECOTT'S
COLLECTION OF PICTURES AND
SONGS

DATE: 1880

LAURENCE HOUSMAN (1865–1959)

*Born in Bromsgrove, UK. Studied at
Lambeth School of Art and the Royal College
of Art. He began work as a book illustrator,
but when his eyesight began to fail, turned to
writing adult books, plays and fairy stories,
which he illustrated himself, and published a
great deal on feminism, socialism and pacifism.
His bold use of black and white shows the
influence of Aubrey Beardsley, but he was also
influenced by the social realism of Dante
Gabriel Rossetti and others of the Pre-
Raphaelite Brotherhood. Books illustrated
include his own* The Blue Moon *(1904),
Christina Rossetti's* Goblin Market *(1893)
and Shelley's* The Sensitive Plant *(1898).*

1—4 *BOOK:*
THE FIELD OF CLOVER

DATE: 1898

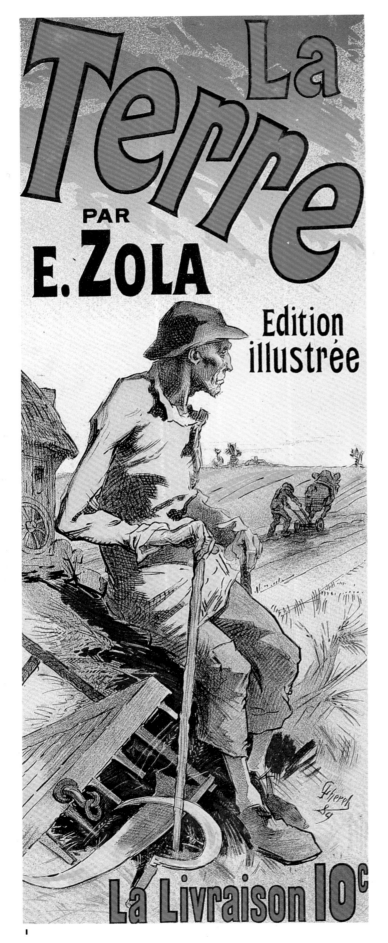

1

2

3

4

5

6

JULES CHERET (1836–1932)

Born in Paris. After working as a lithographer he moved to London in 1859, to study the new techniques of printing in colour lithography being developed there, and earned his living designing book covers for Cramer Publishing and posters for the opera, circus and music hall. He also met and became the protégé of the perfumer Eugène Rimmel. In 1866 Rimmel provided the financial backing for Chéret to set up his own lithographic printing studio in Paris, from where he produced the first French posters printed in colour. His pioneering work in the development of chromolithography enabled the mass-production of posters and contributed to the development of the advertising poster as an artistic medium. His own posters capture the joie de vivre of the cabarets, music and dance halls, operas and theatres of Paris. He designed posters for the American dancer Loïe Fuller for her début at the Folies-Bergère, and his many images of lively dancing girls were popularly known as "Chérettes".

1 *PUBLICITY POSTER:* LA TERRE *by Emile Zola*	
DATE: 1889	
2 *POSTER:* "LOÏE FULLER"	
DATE: 1893	
3 *POSTER:* "PALAIS DE GLACE"	
DATE: 1896	
4 *POSTER:* "JARDIN DE PARIS"	
DATE: 1890	
5 *POSTER:* "THEATRE DE L'OPERA"	
DATE: c. 1896	
6 *POSTER:* "DANSEUSES ESPAGNOLES"	
DATE: c. 1896	

KATE GREENAWAY (1846—1901)

Born in London. Studied at Heatherley's and the Slade School of Art, and began her career illustrating greetings cards. In 1877 she met the printer Edmund Evans, for whom she wrote and illustrated Under the Window *(1878). This was a great success and was followed by, among others,* The Birthday Book *(1880),* The Marigold Garden *(1885) and* The Pied Piper of Hamelin *(1888). She was encouraged in her career by John Ruskin, whom she befriended in 1882 and who, along with Gauguin and the public at large, was a great admirer of her simple style and nostalgic view of childhood.*

1 *PAINTING*
DATE: c. 1899

2 *FRONTISPIECE:*
THE MARIGOLD GARDEN
by Kate Greenaway
DATE: 1885

3 *BOOK:* MOTHER GOOSE
DATE: 1881

Tell Tale Tit,
Your tongue shall be slit;
And all the dogs in the town
Shall have a little bit.

1

2

PHIL MAY (1864–1903)

Born in Leeds, UK. He left school at 13 and became an assistant scene painter at the Leeds Grand Theatre, where he sold his drawings of the actors and actresses for a shilling each. At 14 he started drawing for the Yorkshire Post *and at 16 moved to London, where he contributed to* St Stephen's Review. *He then emigrated to Australia and worked for three years on the* Sydney Bulletin. *Returning penniless to London, he started the highly successful "Parson and Painter" series for* St Stephen's Review, *which was published as a series of annuals from 1891- 1904. He also drew for many periodicals, including* The Graphic, The Daily Graphic *and* The Sketch. *In 1895 he joined the staff of* Punch, *where he remained until his death. Sometimes referred to as the "grandfather of British illustration", he was regarded by many as the most important and influential black-and-white artist of his generation. He lived a bohemian life and died of cirrhosis of the liver and TB at the age of 39.*

1 *ADVERTISEMENT:*
APOLLINARIS TABLE WATER

DATE: c. 1899

2 *MAGAZINE:* THE GRAPHIC

DATE: 1893

1

2

3

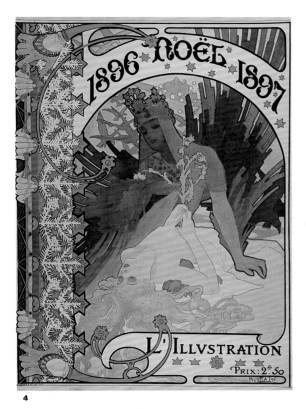

ALPHONSE MUCHA (1860—1939)

Born in Czechoslovakia. Count Karl Khuen-Belasi commissioned him to paint a series of murals for his country home, and subsequently financed Mucha's studies at the Munich Academy. The Count's suicide in 1889 was a financial blow to Mucha, and he turned to illustrating books and journals to make a living. His rise to fame as a leading Art Nouveau designer began with a commission in 1894 to design a poster for Sarah Bernhardt in her leading role in Gismonda. The poster so delighted Bernhardt that she gave Mucha a six-year contract to design posters, stage sets, costumes, jewellery and programmes for her productions. During his career Mucha designed many posters and decorative panels, typically featuring maidens in flowing robes surrounded by formalized decorative symbols. Between 1904 and 1912 he taught in New York and Chicago, where his work appeared in The New York Daily News and The Century magazine.

1 *POSTER:* "LES AMANTS"

DATE: 1895

2 *POSTER:* "AU CAFÉ-CONCERT"

DATE: 1900

3 *POSTER:* "SARAH BERNHARDT"

DATE: c. 1900

4 *MAGAZINE COVER:*
L'ILLUSTRATION

DATE: 1896

5 *ADVERTISEMENT:* "JOB"

DATE: c. 1890

6 *ADVERTISEMENT:*
RUINART CHAMPAGNE

DATE: c. 1890

49

HENRI DE TOULOUSE-LAUTREC
(1864–1901)

Born in Albi, France. His early talent for drawing was encouraged by his uncle and two family friends, the sporting painters René Princeteau and John Lewis Brown. After studying art under Florentin Léon Bonnat and at the school of Fernand Cormon (where he met Vincent van Gogh) he was given an allowance in 1885 to set up his own studio in the Montmartre district of Paris. There he produced his brilliant series of posters, paintings and drawings depicting popular singers, dancers and scenes of Parisian nightlife. Lautrec admired the work of Degas and Gauguin, and the current fashion for Japanese art inspired his daring layouts, bold outlines and solid blocks of colour. In addition to his posters, he produced over 300 lithographs. He also contributed to Courrier Français *and other Paris newspapers, and illustrated Jules Renard's* Histoires Naturelles *(1899).*

1	*POSTER:* "DIVAN JAPONAIS"
	DATE: 1892
2	*POSTER:* "MAY BELFORT"
	DATE: 1895
3	*POSTER:* "LA GOULUE"
	DATE: 1892
4	*MAGAZINE:* LE RIRE
	DATE: 1895
5	*MAGAZINE:* LE RIRE
	DATE: 1896

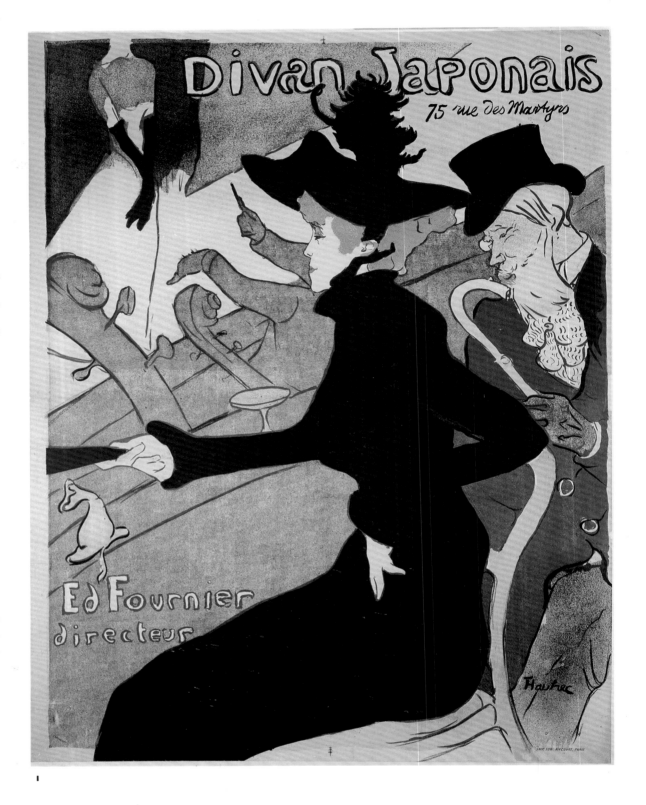

1

2

3

4

5

HABLOT KNIGHT BROWNE
(1815–1882)

Born in London. He was apprenticed to an engraver and subsequently opened a studio of his own and attended St Martin's Lane School. Using the name "Phiz", he illustrated most of the novels of Dickens, including Pickwick Papers *(1836),* Little Dorrit *(1857) and* Nicholas Nickleby *(1839). He contributed to various magazines, including* New Sporting Magazine, London Magazine, The Illustrated Times, Punch *and* The Illustrated London Magazine.

I *BOOK:* LITTLE DORRIT
by Charles Dickens

DATE: 1857

HENRY HOLIDAY (1839–1927)

Born in London. Studied at Leigh's Academy and the Royal Academy Schools. His interest in the Pre-Raphaelite Brotherhood led to his befriending Holman Hunt and Burne-Jones, who had a major influence on his work. He is best known as a stained glass artist, but achieved fame as an illustrator for his illustrations for Lewis Carroll's The Hunting of the Snark *(1876).*

I–4 *BOOK:*
THE HUNTING OF THE SNARK
by Lewis Carroll

DATE: 1876

I

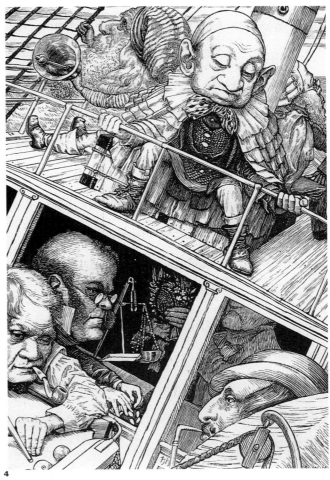

PIERRE BONNARD (1867—1947)

Born in Paris. Studied painting at the Académie Julien in Paris in the late 1880s. With fellow students, including Maurice Denis and Edouard Vuillard, he founded the Nabis, a group of artists with a shared interest in the graphic and decorative arts. In 1891 Bonnard's first commercial poster, France-Champagne, *was published. Thereafter, posters, prints and book illustrations constituted a major part of his work for a number of years. His graphic oeuvre includes a set of lithographs entitled* Aspects of the Life of Paris *and illustrations for, among other works, Jules Renard's* Histoires Naturelles *(1904) and Octave Mirbeau's* La 628 E 8 *(1908), an account of an automobile trip through Europe. Subsequently Bonnard returned to the preoccupations of pure painting and is best known for the work of his later years, interior scenes suffused with colour and light.*

1 *EXHIBITION POSTER:*
"THE PRINT AND THE POSTER"

DATE: 1897

2 *POSTER:* "SALON DES CENT"

DATE: 1896

3 *ADVERTISEMENT:* LE FIGARO

DATE: c. 1899

"The enjoyment of Elinor's company"
Chapter XLIX

1

"You are extremely kind" replied Miss Bates.
Chapter XIX

2

"Of all the consequence in their power"
Chapter XX

3

CHARLES EDMUND BROCK
(1870—1938)

Born in Cambridge, UK. Educated at Cambridge School and in the studio of the sculptor Henry Wiles. He shared a studio with his younger brother, Henry Matthew, and their work was very similar, although Charles' use of line was more tentative. They were equally successful and during their careers illustrated most of the classics, conjuring up images of "the good old days" in the manner of Hugh Thomson. Charles began illustrating in 1891 and his first major commission was for Thomas Hood's Humorous Poems *(1893), which was very popular and led to his most successful book, Swift's* Gulliver's Travels *(1894).*

1 *BOOK:*
SENSE AND SENSIBILITY
by Jane Austen

DATE: 1898

2 *BOOK:* PERSUASION
by Jane Austen

DATE: 1898

3 *BOOK:* EMMA
by Jane Austen

DATE: 1898

AFTER THE DECADENCE OF THE FIN DE SIÈCLE Britain entered the 20th century with a fascination for the decorative arts, which found the perfect medium in the Edwardian gift book.

Many of these were children's stories, but the Net Book Agreement in 1900 had put an end to the booksellers' price war, and the increased cost of these volumes ensured that many if not most of them were for adult entertainment and not destined to suffer the clumsy attentions of boisterous children. Besides which, the subject matter was not of primary importance as the overriding concern was with the decorative possibilities of the book as a whole and not with a close interpretation of the text.

The influence of Art Nouveau and Japanese art was extremely marked throughout this period, and the legacy of Aubrey Beardsley, who died in 1898 at the tragically young age of 23, continued to inspire. Beardsley's works were perfectly suited to the line block process, and there are those who believe he had no peers and that his style died with him. However, in the first decades of the 20th century, one can see his inspiration at work in the drawings of such artists as Alastair, Kay Nielson, Harry Clarke, Edmund Dulac and, to a lesser extent, Arthur Rackham, whose sepia-toned drawings have become definitive of the period.

While Britain and Europe were in the grip of Art Nouveau, America was enjoying its own "golden age of illustration". In the 1890s Howard Pyle had injected a new lease of life into an otherwise dull period of children's illustration with his all-action, black-and-white drawings of adventure on the high seas. His pirate stories were immensely popular, and his prolific output was made possible by his habit of dictating the narrative to his secretary while working on the artwork at his easel.

However, Pyle's fame now rests more on the colour illustrations he did for magazines such as *Harper's* and on the extent of his influence as a teacher, a role that has earned him the title "the father of American illustration". He set up his own school at Chadd's Ford, Pennsylvania, where his star pupils were N C Wyeth, who produced a classic edition of *Treasure Island*, and Frank Schoonover, who inherited Pyle's Pre-Raphaelite obsession with authenticity as well as his love of the Wild West. But the influence of the Pyle school extended way beyond his pupils, and artists like Fred Remington travelled extensively to record the lives of trappers, cowboys and outbackers with a truthful and not romantic eye.

Of course, at that time America was also producing prominent artists who were outside of Pyle's sphere of influence—two examples being Maxfield Parrish and Charles Dana Gibson.

Parrish worked mainly for the major American magazines: *Harper's*, *Collier's*, *The Century* and *Life*. But the experimental nature of his work is beautifully captured in his illustrations for Kenneth Graham's *The Golden Age*, in which, using photographs as reference material, he recreated a child's view of the world by drawing it from a low eye level.

Charles Dana Gibson specialized in pen drawings of fashionable young women and his "Gibson Girls" made him famous and extremely rich. In 1904 *Collier's Weekly* offered him a four-year contract worth $100,000 (about £500,000 in today's terms). When you consider the staggering size of such a fee it is hardly surprising that magazines attracted the cream of American illustrative talent.

Throughout this period, while Europe dominated the field of book production, American publishers favoured the magazine. From an investor's point of view they were a safer bet, as sales could be predicted from fairly stable circulation figures, and the United States had superior technology that could withstand the constant pressure of deadlines while maintaining high standards of colour reproduction.

Gibson's eminence in this milieu is interesting, as it limited his interest to a particular subject matter. In the first decades of the 20th century, on both sides of the Atlantic, this sort of specialization became increasingly commonplace among illustrators. One only has to think of Louis Wain's cats, George Studdy's dogs, Cecil Aldin's horses, Bateman's outraged generals, J A Shepherd's animals clothed in human attire or Mabel Lucie Attwell's rosy-cheeked children to wonder whether this limiting of vision was a condition of the artist's imagination or the force of commerce sustaining a winning formula.

Certainly times were hard for most illustrators, and the arrival of poster and print advertising was a welcome opportunity for diversification. The economic depression after World War I led to a decline in the illustrated book market, but the 1920s and 1930s, particularly in Europe, saw dramatic developments in advertising art.

In Britain, Jack Beddington, the publicity manager of Shell, instigated some of the most famous advertising of all time and became an influential patron of the arts by commissioning the likes of Graham Sutherland, E McKnight Kauffer and Tom Purvis. On the Continent, advertising posters reached dizzying aesthetic heights in the work of the Futurist-inspired A M Cassandre.

This need for artists to find new outlets and media for their talents had been encouraged by the two World Wars. Propaganda to support these war efforts had been in heavy demand and some artists, such as James Montgommery Flagg in America, had become famous becaue of it. At the same time these conflicts encouraged the development of political and social satire, and illustration was broadly used to strengthen the voice of protest.

By the beginning of the 1940s the diversification of illustration had led the artist into every realm of human activity.

CHAPTER TWO
1900-1939

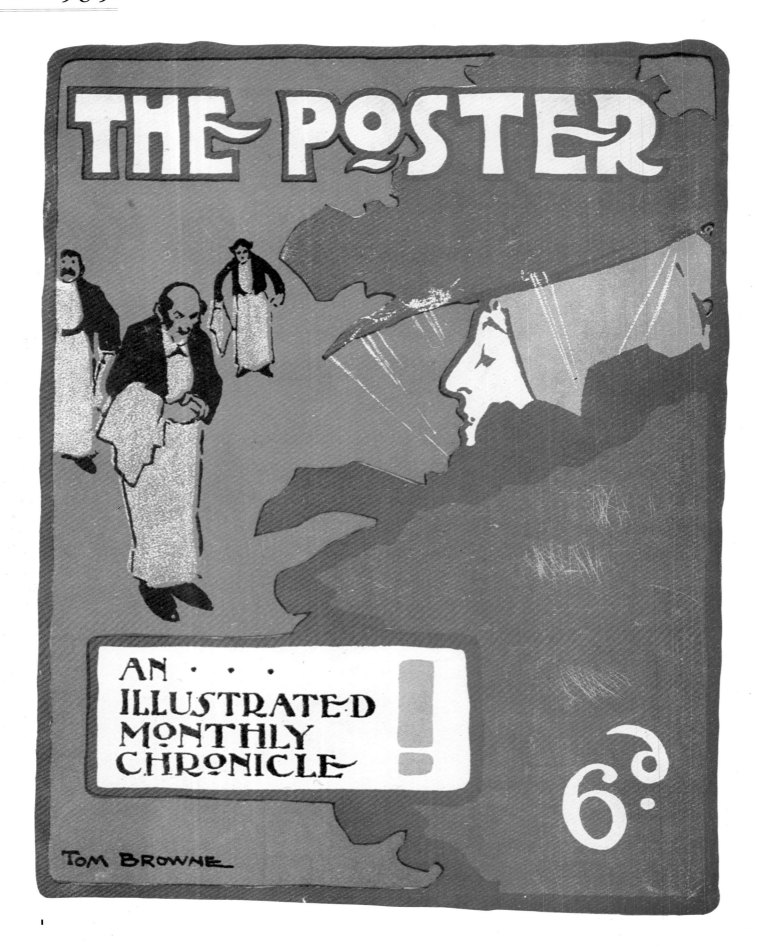

DEAF OLD LADY —
"AH! I CAN DISTINCTLY
HEAR A BEE
HUMMING, SOMEWHERE."

2

3

See their Eyes, as she buys FRY'S.

"EYES FRONT"

TOM BROWNE (1872—1910)

Born in Nottingham, UK. He left school at 11 to work as an errand boy for a local milliner and in 1886 was apprenticed to a firm of lithographic printers for no pay. After a year he was earning one shilling a week. At 17, he became interested in cartoons and sent drawings to the editor of Scraps *comic, which earned him 30 shillings. At 19 he moved to London, where he invented the popular "Weary Willie" and "Tired Tim" comic characters and went on to work for the weekly illustrated papers and* Punch. *He was a member of the Royal Society of British Artists and founder-member of the London Sketch Club. From 1904 he also enjoyed some success in the USA with a series of comic characters called "Boston Types". He contributed to numerous magazines, including* Cycling, The Wheel *and* Cycle Magazine, *and designed posters for Raleigh bicycles. He is most famous for his advertising poster for Johnnie Walker Whisky.*

I *MAGAZINE:* THE POSTER
DATE: c. 1900

2 *ADVERTISEMENT:* FRY'S CHOCOLATE
DATE: c. 1905

3 *ADVERTISEMENT:* FRY'S CHOCOLATE
DATE: c. 1900

4 *ADVERTISEMENT:* BEECHAM'S PILLS
DATE: c. 1905

BEATRIX POTTER (1866—1943)

Born in London. She was entirely self-taught as a watercolourist and displayed a natural gift for drawing animals from a very early age. Her first book, The Tale of Peter Rabbit, *was turned down by several publishers, including her subsequent publishers Frederick Warne and Co., before she published it at her own expense in 1901. She published* The Tailor of Gloucester *the following year. Frederick Warne then published revised versions with illustrations in colour and followed them with* The Tale of Benjamin Bunny *(1904) and* The Tale of Tom Kitten *(1907). Nineteen books in the* Peter Rabbit *series were to follow. Beatrix Potter's little books, with their delicate watercolour vignettes and small blocks of text, have become part of English nursery folklore. Her animals, though endowed with human attributes and dressed in clothes, are nevertheless real because they are sharply observed from nature. She cited the Pre-Raphaelites and Randolph Caldecott as major influences, and admired Mrs Blackburn's bird and animal illustrations as well as Thomas Bewick's woodcuts.*

1, 2 *BOOK:*
THE TALE OF PETER RABBIT

DATE: 1901

3, 5 *BOOK:*
THE TAILOR OF GLOUCESTER

DATE: 1902

4 *BOOK:*
THE TALE OF TOM KITTEN

DATE: 1907

6 *BOOK:*
THE TALE OF BENJAMIN BUNNY

DATE: 1904

1

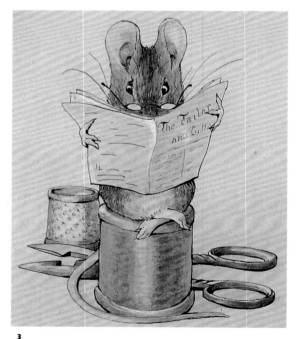

2

3

4

5

6

CHARLES DANA GIBSON
(1867–1944)

Born in Massachusetts, U.S.A. Studied at the Art Students League in New York and at the Académie Julien in Paris. Gibson quickly became an international figure, famous for his drawings chronicling American high society, and created a beautiful type of all-American girl, known as "the Gibson Girl". He sold his first drawing to Life *magazine when he was 19, beginning a lifelong association which culminated in his becoming its owner and editor after World War I. An early admirer of Abbey, Frost and Pyle, he later developed a special liking for the British illustrators Charles Keene, George du Maurier and Phil May. He was President of the Society of Illustrators during World War I.*

1, 2 *BOOK:* AMERICANS
by Charles Dana Gibson

DATE: 1901

1

2

1

2

3

4

5

DEAN CORNWELL (1892–1960)

Cornwell was a student of Harvey Dunn, through whom he inherited much of the teaching of Howard Pyle, and he also studied under the muralist Frank Brangwyn. Although obviously an exponent of the Pyle school, Cornwell's style was more elaborately decorative. He worked in oils and was painstaking in his approach to the subject, making many preliminary sketches, and throughout the 1920s his beautiful illustrations of swashbuckling, romantic costume dramas dominated such magazines as Redbook *and* Cosmopolitan. *However, it was Norman Rockwell's belief that Cornwell's best work was a series on the life of Christ, for* Good Housekeeping, *which he painted after a trip to the Middle East. His murals are no less impressive than his illustrations, the most notable being those for the Los Angeles Public Library, the Lincoln Memorial in California and the Tennessee State Office Building. He taught illustration at the Art Students League in New York, where he created the "Cornwell School", and had a profound influence on such artists as Harry Beckhoff, Dan Content, Rico Tomaso, Robert Benney and Frank Reilly. From 1922-26 he was President of the Society of Illustrators and was elected to its Hall of Fame in 1959.*

1 *MAGAZINE:* COSMOPOLITAN	
DATE: 1923	
2 *DRAWING:* WWI "DOUGHBOY"	
DATE: c. 1918	
3 *MAGAZINE:* COSMOPOLITAN	
DATE: c. 1918	
4 *PAINTING*	
DATE: 1938	
5 *MAGAZINE:* COSMOPOLITAN	
DATE: 1923	

EDWARD JULIUS DETMOLD
(1883–1957)

Born in London. Edward and his twin brother Charles Maurice started drawing in early childhood and, though neither had received any formal training, both exhibited at the Royal Academy from the age of 14. They collaborated on several books, including Pictures from Birdland *(1899) and Kipling's* The Jungle Book *(1903), until Charles Maurice committed suicide in 1908 at the age of 25. Alone, Edward illustrated* The Fables of Aesop *(1909),* Fabres Book of Insects *(1921) and* The Arabian Nights *(Tales From One Thousand and One Nights) (1924), which shows the strong influence of Japanese prints and Eastern miniature painting. He specialized in drawing animals and plants, often placed in fantastical settings.*

1, 2 *BOOK:* THE JUNGLE BOOK
by Rudyard Kipling

DATE: 1903

3 *BOOK:* HOURS OF GLADNESS
by M Maeterlinck

DATE: 1912

4, 5 *BOOK:*
OUR LITTLE NEIGHBOURS,
ANIMALS OF THE FARM AND
WOOD

DATE: 1921

1

2

3

4

5

1

CHARLES MARION RUSSELL
(1864—1926)

*Born in Missouri, USA. Russell's childhood
interest in drawing cowboys and Indians was
to shape his life. He left school at 16 and
worked as a cowboy, then as a fur-trapper. In
1888 he spent six months living with the
Blackfoot Indians and learned to communicate
with them in sign language. As an artist he
was entirely self-taught. His wife Nancy
encouraged him to become a full-time
illustrator, handling his finances and
organizing his commissions. His work
appeared in many magazines, including*
Recreation, Western Field, Sports Afield
and Outing, *and he later contributed to*
Scribner's, McClures *and* The Saturday
Evening Post. *A contemporary of Fred
Remington, his beautifully coloured paintings
captured the spirit of the life he depicted and
showed a remarkable understanding of animal
anatomy. He was elected posthumously to the
Illustrators' Hall of Fame in 1985.*

1 *PAINTING:*
"COWBOYS ROPING A STEER"

DATE: c. 1900

2 *PAINTING:*
"COWBOYS ROPING A STEER"

DATE: 1904

2

JAMES A SHEPHERD
(1867–c. 1940)

Born in London. He had no formal training, but learned his art while working for the magazine Moonshine, *developing a particular talent for drawing birds and animals in pen and ink, which became his speciality. Although comic and usually clothed in human attire, his creatures are nevertheless entirely plausible characters — his illustrations for* Uncle Remus *(1901) being excellent examples. He had a long association with* Punch *magazine from 1893 and drew for several other magazines, including* The Sporting and Dramatic News *and* Cassell's Family Magazine. *His caricatures for* The Strand Magazine, *known as "Zig-Zags", proved so popular that they were subsequently published as a book,* Zig-Zag Fables, *in 1897. Other books include* The Three Jovial Puppies *(1907) and* The Life of a Foxhound *(1910).*

1—3 *BOOK:* UNCLE REMUS
by J Chandler Harris

DATE: 1901

1

2

3

4

HARRY ROUNTREE (1878–1950)

Born in Auckland, New Zealand, the son of a banker. He worked as a lithographer before moving to London in 1901. His humorous drawings of animals and children were commissioned by Little Folks, The Humorist, Playtime *and* Punch. *He became one of the most successful children's illustrators of his day and in 1914 was President of the London Sketch Club. Books illustrated include* Alice in Wonderland *(1908),* Alice Through the Looking Glass *(1928) and* The Magic Wand *(1908). Among his own works were* Birds, Beasts and Fishes *(1929) and* Rabbit Rhymes *(1934). He also illustrated for magazines such as* The Sketch, The Graphic *and* The Strand Magazine.

1—4 *BOOK:* UNCLE REMUS *by J Chandler Harris*	
DATE: 1906	
5 *ORIGINAL PRINT*	
DATE: NOT KNOWN	
6, 7 *BOOK:* AESOP'S FABLES	
DATE: 1924	

5

6

7

Christian passes through the Valley of the Shadow of Death.

2

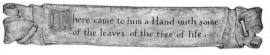

There came to him a Hand with some of the leaves of the tree of life.

3

Christian and Hopeful under the power of Giant Despair.

4

Christian on his way to Legality's house.

5

FRANK C PAPE (1878–1972)

Little biographical detail is known about this artist, but he was a prolific illustrator with an expert understanding of the various reproduction media. His finely drawn line work appeared in The Children of the Dawn *(1908),* The Book of Psalms *(1912) and* The Story Without an End *(1912). He illustrated classics from* The Pilgrim's Progress *(1910) to* Tales from the Arabian Nights *(1934) and also contemporary novels, and contributed to* The Boy's Herald, Cassell's Magazine *and* The Pall Mall Magazine. *His illustrations to six works by Anatole France, produced in the 1920s, are regarded as among his finest and he became something of a cult figure during that period. His wife, Agnes Stringer, collaborated with him on some projects, providing the colour work to his drawings.*

I *BOOK:*
THE PEDLAR AND HIS DOG
by Mary C Rowsell

DATE: 1922

2—5 *BOOK:*
THE PILGRIM'S PROGRESS
by John Bunyan

DATE: c. 1909

LOUIS WAIN (1860–1939)

*Born in London. Attended the West London
School of Art, 1877-80, and taught there
during the following two years. Encouraged by
his wife, Emily, he sold his first drawing of a
cat (based on his own, Peter) to* The
Illustrated London News *in 1884. His first
book,* Madam Tabby's Establishment
*(1886), made him a household name as "the
man who drew cats", and in 1890 he was
made President of the National Cat Club,
devising their coat of arms and motto. From
1890, Wain invented a world of "humanized"
cats, sporting top hats and monocles, playing
tennis and drinking tea. The public loved
them, and Wain was approached to illustrate
countless books, articles and picture postcards.
In 1907 he went to New York, where he drew
a cat strip cartoon for* New York American.
In 1917 he produced an animated film,
Pussyfoot, *with the pioneer film-maker H F
Wood. The first* Louis Wain Annual
*appeared in 1901 and annuals appeared
regularly until 1921, when the public appetite
for Wain's drawings diminished. Diagnosed as
schizophrenic at the age of 63, he spent his last
years at the Royal Bethlem Hospital in south
London.*

1 "CATS' TEA PARTY"	
(unpublished)	
DATE: c. 1910	
2 "THE CHAIRMAN"	
(unpublished)	
DATE: c. 1910	
3 *POSTCARD*	
DATE: NOT KNOWN	

1

FIRMIN BOUISSET
(1859—1925)

*Born in Mossac, France. Brother of the artist
Felix François Bouisset, he was a painter,
engraver and illustrator. His style was very
much of the Art Nouveau period and he is best
remembered for his paintings of children and
for his posters, most notably those for Meunier
chocolate and Job papers. His work also
appeared in the publications* Le Capitan
(1833) and L'Estampe Moderne *(1899)
and his illustrated books include* La Journée
de Bébé *(1885) and* Les Bébés d'Alsace de
Lorraine *(1886). He died in Paris at the age
of 66.*

1 "LA BOUQUETIÈRE"
(unpublished)

DATE: c. 1900

2 *POSTER:*
"LONDON COUNTRY &
WESTMINSTER BANK (PARIS) LTD"

DATE: 1919

3 *ADVERTISEMENT:*
"CHOCOLAT DE L'UNION"

DATE: c. 1900

2

3

HOWARD PYLE (1853–1911)

Born in Delaware, USA, and educated at the Art Students League in New York. Pyle is often referred to as "the father of American illustration", because of the enormous influence both of his work and his teaching. He taught at the Drexel Institute in Philadelphia and then at the Art Students League in New York before setting up his own art schools at Chadd's Ford, Pennsylvania, and Wilmington, Delaware, where no fees were charged. Some of his star pupils included N C Wyeth, Frank Schoonover and Jessie Wilcox Smith. Books illustrated include The Merry Adventures of Robin Hood *(1883), a series of books which he also wrote, re-telling the legends of King Arthur, and* Book of Pirates *(1902). He also contributed to a number of magazines, including* Harpers.

1—3 *BOOK:*
HOWARD PYLE'S BOOK OF
PIRATES

DATE: 1902

4 *MAGAZINE:*
HARPER'S MONTHLY

DATE: 1911

5 *MAGAZINE:*
HARPER'S MONTHLY

DATE: 1906

2

3

4

5

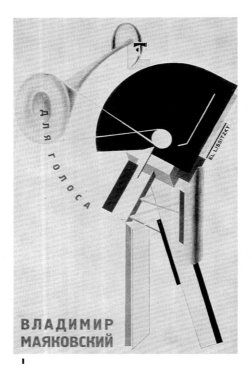

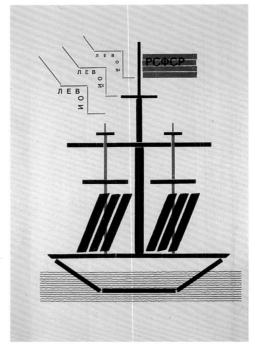

EL LISSITZKY (1890–1941)

Born in Smolensk, Russia. Studied in Germany and took up book illustration on his return to Russia in 1912. He illustrated seven children's books, including The Kid *(1917), which revealed the influence of Marc Chagall,* Ukrainian Fairy Tales *(1919) and* The Four Billygoats *(1924). In 1919 he entered what he termed his "Proun" period — the name he gave to his abstract style and which was an acronym meaning "Project for the Establishment of the New Art". In 1920 he produced* Of Two Squares, *an abstract play book for children that showed a red square attacking and defeating a black square. In 1921 he returned to Germany, where he was deeply impressed by the Dadaists and Expressionists, and in 1925 wrote* The Isms of Art *with Hans Arp. Throughout his career he was a highly influential political artist, famous for his posters and his geometric use of typography. He designed the first flag of the Central Committee of the Communist Party of the Soviet Union and between 1932 and 1937 created a series of montages called "Building the USSR", which bring to mind the work of John Heartfield.*

1, 2 *BOOK: (published in Russia)*

DATE: 1923

3 *BOOK: (published in Russia)*

DATE: 1916

The Banquet

1

WILL H BRADLEY (1868–1962)

Born in Boston, USA. He started work at the age of 12 on a Michigan newspaper and in 1895 illustrated his first book, Fringilla *by R D Blackmore, which clearly shows the influence of Beardsley and Art Nouveau. In the same year he founded his own Wayside Press Company, in Springfield, Massachusetts, and developed his interest in typography and book design. He wrote, illustrated and produced* Peter Poodle: Toy Maker to the King *(1906) and* Launcelot and the Ladies *(1927). He was also a talented poster designer, and was art director of* Collier's, Metropolitan *and* The Century *magazines.*

I *BOOK:* PETER POODLE: TOY MAKER TO THE KING	
DATE: 1906	
2 *POSTER*	
DATE: c. 1920	
3 *BOOK JACKET:* THE CHAP BOOK *by Will Bradley*	
DATE: NOT KNOWN	

2

3

LUDWIG HOHLWEIN (1874–1949)

Born in Wiesbaden, Germany. Trained as an architect and practised until 1906, with a special interest in exhibition design. He was self-taught as an artist, but his first poster design, a sporting guns advertisement, won him immediate recognition. His personal interest in hunting, field sports and animal life was frequently reflected in the style and content of his commercial work. Whether for tailoring or perfumes, tobacco or confectionery, or the circus, his posters show his confident handling of form, colour and pattern, assembled into bold and inventive imagery. In a poster for Grathwohl cigarettes (1921), the product is represented only by a tiny red glow at the mouth of a silhouetted figure; frequently figures appear as outlined shapes filled with solid blocks of colour and pattern. In later work, high tonal contrasts and a network of interlocking shapes provide modelling of three-dimensional forms. His style is unmistakable and was powerfully adapted to propagandist posters in both World Wars.

1 *ADVERTISEMENT:* PKZ

DATE: 1908

2 *ADVERTISEMENT:*
MACHOLL COGNAC

DATE: c. 1910

3 *ADVERTISEMENT:* RIQUETTA

DATE: c. 1910

4 *WWI POSTER:*
"THE LUDENDORFF FUND FOR
THE WAR WOUNDED"

DATE: 1917

1

2

3

4

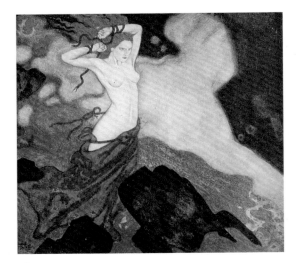

1

2

EDMUND DULAC (1882–1953)

*Born in Toulouse, France. He took evening
classes in art while studying law at Toulouse
University, and won a scholarship to the
Académie Julien in Paris, but left after three
weeks to concentrate on his career as an
illustrator. He was an Anglophile from
childhood (his nickname at school was
"l'Anglais") and settled in London in 1905. By
the time he became a naturalized British
subject in 1912, he was established as one of the
leading artists in his field. During World War I
he designed charity stamps and later Jubilee
and Coronation stamps and was commissioned
by Charles de Gaulle to design posters, bank
notes and postage stamps. He was a friend of
W B Yeats, many of whose works he
illustrated, and collaborated with him on a
production of* At the Hawk's Well,
*composing the music and designing the
costumes, sets and make-up. Books illustrated
include* Stories of the Arabian Nights,
retold by Laurence Housman (1907),
Shakespeare's The Tempest *(1908),* Stories
from Hans Christian Andersen *(1911) and
the novels of the Brontë sisters in ten volumes
(1905). Dulac's brilliant use of flat colour owes
a great deal to the influence of Japanese prints
and his passionate interest in Persian
miniatures.*

1 *BOOK:* KING ALBERT

DATE: 1914

2 *PAINTING:*
"THE ENTOMOLOGIST"

DATE: 1909

3 *BOOK:* THE MERMAID KING
by Hans Christian Andersen

DATE: 1911

4 *CARICATURE:* SIR EDWARD
PENISON ROSS

DATE: 1915

3

4

HENRY MATTHEW BROCK
(1875–1960)

*Born in Cambridge, UK, younger brother of
Charles Edmund Brock. Studied at
Cambridge School of Art. He illustrated for
numerous periodicals, including* The
Graphic, Punch *and* The Sketch. *Books
illustrated include Walter Scott's* Ivanhoe
(1900), Defoe's Robinson Crusoe *(1904),
Hans Andersen's* Fairy Tales and Stories
(1905), Dent's The Novels of Jane Austen
and R L Stevenson's Treasure Island
*(1928). He also designed posters for the
D'Oyly Carte during the 1920s. Brock worked
almost entirely in pen and ink. His flair for
drama and action, and his fluent and vigorous
line, made him popular as an illustrator of
boys' stories. He was described by the
illustrator A E Bestall as "probably the last of
the era of perfectionists".*

1–3 *BOOK:*
THE BOOK OF FAIRY TALES

DATE: 1914

1

2

3

1

2

THE LONDON UNITED TRAMWAYS

T^HE PHEASANT AT HOME

TO PAY YOUR RESPECTS
TRAVEL BY TRAM TO THE

BUCKINGHAMSHIRE WOODS AT
UXBRIDGE

3

THE LONDON UNITED TRAMWAYS

T^HE KINGFISHER AT HOME

TO PAY YOUR RESPECTS
TRAVEL BY TRAM TO THE
RIVERSIDE AT . . . . .

HAMPTON COURT OR
KEW BRIDGE

4

ERNEST ARIS (1882–1963)

*Born in Bradford, UK. Studied at Bradford
School of Art and the Royal College of Art,
London. He began work as a portrait painter
but went on to a successful career as an
illustrator of children's books. He contributed
illustrations to children's stories in* The
Graphic *and book titles include* Tales for
Tiny Tots *and* The Rock-a-Bye Stories
(1919), The Woodland Series *(1919),*
Famous Animal Tales *(1935) and* The
Brambledown Tales *(1946). His work was
published in the USA, Canada and Australia
as well as in the UK.*

| 1 *BOOK:* THE TREASURE SEEKERS |
| *by E Nesbit* |
| *DATE:* 1917 |

| 2 *BOOK:* |
| THE HOUSE THAT JACK BUILT |
| *(traditional rhyme)* |
| *DATE:* 1920 |

| 3 *POSTER:* |
| LONDON UNITED TRAMWAYS |
| *DATE:* 1915 |

| 4 *POSTER:* |
| LONDON UNITED TRAMWAYS |
| *DATE:* 1915 |

ROBERT ANNING BELL
(1863–1933)

*Born in London. Trained at Westminster
School of Art and the Royal Academy Schools.
He also studied under Sir George Frampton in
England and Morot in Paris. Books illustrated
include* Jack the Giant Killer and Beauty
and the Beast *and* The Sleeping Beauty
and Dick Whittington *(both published in
1894),* Poems *by John Keats (1897),*
Shelley's Poems *(1902),* Shakespeare's The
Tempest *(1901) and, his most successful book,*
A Midsummer Night's Dream *(1895). He
also contributed to* The Yellow Book
*quarterly. Bell's work was firmly rooted in the
Arts and Crafts tradition, often featuring long,
angular figures, without shading, contained
within decorative borders. As well as being an
illustrator, he was also a sculptor and designer
of stained glass and mosaics. (Examples of his
mosaics may be seen at the Houses of
Parliament and at Westminster Cathedral.)
He taught at Liverpool Municipal College, the
Glasgow School of Art and the Royal College
of Art, and became a member of the Royal
Academy in 1922.*

1 *BOOK:*
DAILY CHRONICLE PORTFOLIO

DATE: 1911

2 *BOOKPLATE*

DATE: 1910

3 *BOOK:*
PALGRAVE'S GOLDEN TREASURY

DATE: c. 1914

"DAILY CHRONICLE" PORTFOLIO
OF
HISTORIC SCENES AT CORONATION
OF
KING GEORGE & QUEEN MARY

BY FRANK BRANGWYN A·R·A; JOHN COPLEY; J.M'LURE HAMILTON
A.S.HARTRICK A·R·W·S; F.ERNEST JACKSON; JOSEPH PENNELL
SPENCER PRYSE; E.J.SULLIVAN A·R·W·S; W.L.WYLLIE.R·A
One Guinea

1

2

3

LUCIAN BERNHARD (1883—1972)

Born in Stuttgart, Germany. Mainly self-taught, in 1905 he won a competition sponsored by the Berlin Chamber of Commerce with a poster for Priester matches, an image which set the hallmark of his style — descriptively economical shapes, bold colours and the strong presence of the brand name — later applied to posters for Stiller shoes, Manoli cigarettes, Osram lamps and Adler typewriters. This concentration on the advertised product, eliminating all other elements that might distract, became known as sachplakat *(object-poster). During World War I, Bernhard's expertise was applied to war propaganda posters. In 1920 he became the first Professor of Poster Design at the (then) Royal Academy in Berlin, and with Dr Hans Sachs he established the magazine* Das Plakat. *In 1923 he moved to the USA, where he became a founder-member of the New York design firm Contempora, Inc., with Rockwell Kent and others. His design skills were applied to trademarks, packaging, emblems and printers' ornaments, and he is well known for type design, with 36 typefaces to his credit, including Bernhard-Antiqua and Fraktur.*

1 *WWI POSTER:* WAR LOAN

DATE: 1917

2 *ADVERTISEMENT:*
BENEDICTINE LIQUEUR

DATE: 1921

3 *ADVERTISEMENT:*
OIGEE BINOCULARS

DATE: 1907

EMIL CARDINAUX (1877–1937)

Born in Berne, Switzerland. He began drawing as a child and by the age of 18 he had already illustrated the legend of William Tell. He studied art under Paul Volmars at Berne University and in 1898 studied under Franz Stuck at the Munich Art Academy. He travelled and lived in various parts of Europe and from 1903-04 worked as an artist in France and Italy. His versatile technique enabled him to succeed as a caricaturist, illustrator and poster designer.

1 *TRAVEL POSTER:* ZERMATT

DATE: 1908

2 *TRAVEL POSTER:* DAVOS

DATE: 1918

3 *TRAVEL POSTER:* LOTSCHBERG

DATE: c. 1916

4 *POSTER:* "SWISS COUNTY EXHIBITION, BERNE"

DATE: 1914

1

2

3

4

1

2

3

KAY NIELSEN (1886–1957)

Born in Copenhagen, Denmark. He spent his childhood surrounded by artists, writers and musicians, among them Ibsen and Grieg. His early talent for drawing was encouraged by his parents and at the age of 17 he was sent to the Académie Julien in Paris, where he came under the influence of Art Nouveau, Japanese art, and the work of Aubrey Beardsley. His first commission was for In Powder and Crinoline *(1913), which was later published as* Twelve Dancing Princesses *in the USA. He also illustrated* One Thousand and One Nights *(1918–22),* East of the Sun and West of the Moon *(1914) and* Hans Andersen's Fairy Tales *(1924). Nielsen was a brilliant colourist whose intensely decorative style came under a number of influences, including Beardsley, "Alastair", Vernon Hill, Middle Eastern art and the sculptural effects of the incipient Art Deco. After exhibiting in New York in 1917 he emigrated to the USA in 1922, moving to Hollywood in 1939, where he designed for a number of film companies, including Walt Disney.*

1 *BOOK:* THE KING ALBERT BOOK

DATE: 1914

2, 3 *BOOK:*
IN POWDER AND CRINOLINE

DATE: 1913

MOTHERS-VOTE LABOUR

1

YESTERDAY-THE TRENCHES

2

"WORKLESS"

3

4

HANS RUDI ERDT (b. 1883)

Born in South Bavaria. After leaving grammar school he studied at the Industrial Art College in Munich, where he was the protégé of his professor, Maximilian von Dasio. In 1905 he moved to Berlin, where he became a commercial poster artist. His style tended towards two-dimensional caricatures and his early work shows the influence of Ludwig Hohlwein, whereas in his later drawings one can see his admiration for the compositions and technique of Lucian Bernhard.

1 *POSTER*

DATE: 1917

GERALD SPENCER PRYSE
(1882—1956)

Born in Ashton, UK. He studied art in London and Paris, became a member of the International Society and exhibited at Venice from 1907. He lived in Morocco from 1950 until his death. His illustrations appeared in Punch, The Strand Magazine *and* The Graphic.

1 *POSTER*

DATE: c. 1919

2 *POSTER*

DATE: c. 1919

3 *POSTER*

DATE: c. 1919

4 *POSTER*

DATE: 1924

1

ARTHUR RACKHAM (1867–1939)

*Born in London. Attended evening classes at
Lambeth School of Art while working as a
clerk. By 1891 he was selling illustrations to*
The Pall Mall Gazette, Scraps *and*
Illustrated Bits, *and in 1892 he joined the
staff of* The Westminster Budget
Magazine. *Rackham was one of the foremost
Edwardian book illustrators, specializing in
tales with a mystical, magical or legendary
theme. Until 1905 he was highly regarded as a
line illustrator, but the introduction of colour
printing in the early 1900s enabled him also to
use the subtle tints and muted tones for which
he is now so widely known. He was influenced
by Doyle, Houghton and Beardsley, as well as
the prints of Dürer and Altdorfer. In 1900 he
married the portrait painter Edyth Starkie,
who encouraged him to develop the highly
imaginative and distinctive style with which
he evoked the fantastical image world of
childhood. He illustrated over 50 books,
including* The Fairy Tales of the Brothers
Grimm *(1900),* Rip Van Winkle *(1905),*
Alice in Wonderland *(1907),* The Arthur
Rackham Fairy Book *(1933),* Christina
Rossetti's *Goblin Market (1933),* Edgar
Allan Poe's *Tales of Mystery and
Imagination (1935) and Kenneth Grahame's*
The Wind in the Willows *(1940).*

---

1 *ORIGINAL DESIGN:*
THE HOUSE THAT JACK BUILT
(traditional rhyme)

DATE: 1913

---

2 *BOOK:* PEER GYNT
by Henrik Ibsen

DATE: 1936

---

3 *SOURCE:* NOT KNOWN

DATE: NOT KNOWN

---

4 *BOOK:*
THE NIGHT BEFORE CHRISTMAS
by C C Moore

DATE: 1931

---

5 *BOOK:*
PETER PAN IN KENSINGTON
GARDENS
by J M Barrie

DATE: 1906

2

3

4

5

1

FRED REMINGTON (1861–1909)

Born in New York State. He was educated for a short while at Yale University before going west to work as a cowboy, where he began drawing images of the disappearing Wild West. The early drawings which he sent to Harper's *magazine were published only after being redrawn by staff artists, but his work improved and he eventually joined the magazine staff himself. Books illustrated include* Ranch Life and the Hunting Trail *(1888) by his friend Theodore Roosevelt, and Longfellow's* The Song of Hiawatha *(1891).*

1 *PAINTING:* "STAMPEDED BY LIGHTNING"

DATE: 1908

2 *PAINTING:* "SMOKE SIGNALS"

DATE: 1905

2

EDOUARD ELZINGRE (1880–1966)

Born in Neuenburg, Switzerland. Studied fine art at the art school in La Chaux-de-Fonds under Georges Aubert and at the Académie Julien in Paris. He began his career as an illustrator for various Parisian publishing companies, and from 1906 he illustrated books and worked for the Geneva Tribune newspaper. His favourite themes were circus and racing horses, which he both painted and sculpted. His brilliant use of colour and typography ensured his success as a poster artist and his work for various clients covered a broad range of subjects.

1 *POSTER:*
"20th ANNIVERSARY OF THE
REVIVAL OF THE OLYMPIC
GAMES"

DATE: 1914

2 *TRAVEL POSTER:*
WINTER SPORTS, FRANCE

DATE: 1905

3 *TRAVEL POSTER:*
NEUCHATEL, SWITZERLAND

DATE: 1914

1

'Miss Bates was very chatty and good-humoured.'

2

HUGH THOMSON (1860–1920)

Born in Londonderry, Northern Ireland. He began work at the age of 17 designing Christmas cards for Messrs Marcus Ward in Belfast. He moved to London in 1883 and became a regular contributor to The English Illustrated *magazine. Thomson was a great admirer of E A Abbey, whose influence can be seen in his excellent black-and-white drawings, which perfectly captured the period details of the stories he illustrated. From the mid-1880s, his work graced the pages of novels by authors such as Goldsmith, Jane Austen, Sheridan and Mrs Gaskell. His first major success was Tristram's* Coaching Days and Coaching Ways *(1888), followed in 1891 by the even more successful* Vicar of Wakefield *by Oliver Goldsmith. Other books illustrated include Goldsmith's* She Stoops To Conquer *(1912), J M Barrie's* Quality Street *(1913) and several Shakespeare plays. He also illustrated for most of the major magazines, including* Black & White, The Pall Mall Budget *and* The Graphic. *A pioneer of the new photomechanical process in the early 1900s, Thomson did his best work between 1900 and 1915 and was enormously influential on a whole generation of younger artists.*

1 *BOOK:* QUALITY STREET
by J M Barrie

DATE: 1913

2 *BOOK:* EMMA
by Jane Austen

DATE: c. 1900

3 *BOOK:*
THE MERRY WIVES OF WINDSOR
by William Shakespeare

DATE: 1910

3

1

FLORENCE UPTON (1873–1922)

Born in New York, of English parentage.
Studied in New York, Paris and Holland.
Initially she was a portrait painter, but in
1893 she began making sketches of the wooden
dolls she had played with as a child. She
invented the name "Golliwogg" for her
favourite and in 1895 she illustrated a picture
book of his adventures, with simple rhymes
written by her mother. The Adventures of
Two Dutch Dolls and a Golliwogg, *with its*
brightly coloured whole-page drawings and
hand-written text, was a great success and led
to a series of thirteen Golliwogg books,
including The Golliwogg in War! *(1899)*,
The Golliwogg's Auto Go-Cart *(1901)*
and The Golliwogg's Fox Hunt *(1905)*.
The original manuscripts and the doll itself
were auctioned for charity and are now kept at
Chequers, the country home of British Prime
Ministers.

1 *BOOK:*
THE GOLLIWOGG'S AUTO GO-
CART

DATE: 1901

2 *ADVERTISEMENT:*
WELLINGTON BROMIDE PAPERS

DATE: c. 1910

3 *ADVERTISEMENT:*
WELLINGTON CELLULOID FILM

DATE: c. 1910

2

3

1

HENRIETTE WILLEBEEK
LE MAIR (1889–1966)

*(Baroness H van Tuyll van Serooskerken.)
Born in Rotterdam, Holland. Her parents
were patrons of the arts and, on the advice of
the French illustrator Maurice Boutet de
Monvel (by whose work she was deeply
influenced), she was educated at the
Rotterdam Academy. Her first British book,*
Our Old Nursery Rhymes, *was published in
1911 and over the next two decades her delicate
pastel illustrations of children became
increasingly popular. Her work appeared in*
Old Dutch Nursery Rhymes *(1917), A A
Milne's* A Gallery of Children *(1925) and
R L Stevenson's* A Child's Garden of
Verses *(1926). Her interest in a child's world
extended beyond illustration as she also
designed children's tableware.*

1—3 *BOOK:*
OUR OLD NURSERY RHYMES

DATE: 1911

1 ORANGES AND LEMONS

2 HERE WE GO ROUND THE
MULBERRY BUSH

3 HICKORY DICKORY DOCK

2

3

CHARLES ROBINSON (1870–1937)

Born in London, the brother of William Heath Robinson. He won a scholarship to the Royal Academy Schools but was financially unable to take it up. Instead he worked as an apprentice printer during the day and attended art classes in the evenings. In 1895 his illustrations were printed in The Studio *magazine, which led to his being invited to illustrate R L Stevenson's* A Child's Garden of Verse *(1895). He subsequently illustrated well over a hundred books, mostly for children, including Lewis Carroll's* Alice's Adventures in Wonderland *(1907),* The Big Book of Fairy Tales *(1911) and Oscar Wilde's* The Happy Prince and Other Stories *(1913). He illustrated for magazines including* Black & White, The Graphic, The Queen *and* The Yellow Book. *Robinson painted delicate and sensitive watercolours, and his black and white illustrations, reflecting the influence of Beardsley, Dürer and Walter Crane, made him as famous in his day as Beardsley had been in his.*

1 *BOOK:* THE SENSITIVE PLANT
by Percy Shelley

DATE: 1911

2—4 *BOOK:*
THE HAPPY PRINCE AND OTHER STORIES
by Oscar Wilde

DATE: 1913

JOSEPH PENNELL (1860–1926)

Born in Philadelphia, USA. He worked as a clerk while taking evening classes at the Pennsylvania School of Industrial Art, until he was expelled for leading a student rebellion in 1879. He attended the Pennsylvania Academy of Fine Arts, but left in 1880 to become a freelance illustrator and writer. He married Elizabeth Robins, the authoress, and they settled in England in 1884. There the Pennells wrote a biography of their friend, the artist James McNeill Whistler, and also brought the young illustrator Aubrey Beardsley to public attention with an article on his work in the first edition of The Studio *magazine. Pennell lectured in illustration at the Slade School of Art and the Royal College and won many awards, including gold medals at the Paris and Dresden Expositions. His illustrations appeared in magazines such as* The Yellow Book, The Graphic, The English Illustrated *and* Pall Mall. *Books illustrated include* The Jew At Home *(1892) and Henry James's* A Little Tour in France *(1900), as well as numerous travel books written by his wife.*

1 *WWI POSTER:*
"BUY LIBERTY BONDS"

DATE: 1917

2 *ENGRAVING*

DATE: 1909

3 *ENGRAVING*

DATE: 1911

1

2

3

I

ALASTAIR (1889–1969)

*Real name Baron Hans Henning Voight. Born
in Karlsruhe, Germany. Self-taught as an
artist, he was also a dancer, mime artist,
pianist and writer. His career as a graphic
artist was launched in 1914, when John Lane
published* Forty-Three Drawings by
Alastair. *He also illustrated Oscar Wilde's*
The Sphinx *(1920), Edgar Allan Poe's* The
Fall of the House of Usher *(1928),
Choderlos de Laclos's* Les Liaisons
Dangereuses *(1929) and his own* Fifty
Drawings by Alastair *(1925). Like
Beardsley, whom he greatly admired,
Alastair's illustrations combined decorative
elegance with a fascination for the perverse
and the sinister. His drawings, in black and
white and sometimes coloured ink, were
compositions inspired by novels, poems, plays
or figures of legend or history. He exhibited at
the Weyhe Gallery in New York in 1925.*

❚ *BOOK:* THE SPHINX
by Oscar Wilde

DATE: 1920

FRANK EARLE SCHOONOVER
(1877–1972)

Born in Oxford, New Jersey, USA. Studied under Howard Pyle at the Drexel Institute and then at Pyle's school at Chadd's Ford, Pennsylvania. He studied hard and the influence of Pyle as mentor is evident both in his painterly style and his choice of subject matter. Both men had a love of the colonial past and the Wild West and Schoonover subscribed to Pyle's view that an illustrator must be closely involved with the subject of his work. To this end he travelled widely and in difficult circumstances to record the lives of cowboys, Indians and Eskimos. His work appeared in Arctic Stowaways *(1917),* Ivanhoe *(1922), J W Schultz's* Questers of the Desert *(1925), M P Smith's* Boy Captives of Old Deerfield *(1929) and V M Collier's* Roland the Warrior *(1934), among others.*

1 *PAINTING:* "BELLEAU WOOD"	
DATE: 1918	
2 *ADVERTISEMENT:* COLT'S FIREARMS	
DATE: 1925	
3 *BOOK:* JOAN OF ARC	
DATE: 1920	

1

2

3

JESSIE MARION KING (1876–1949)

Born in Scotland. Studied at Glasgow School of Art, where she later taught, and at the Royal College of Art in London. An early member of the "Glasgow School", with Charles Rennie Mackintosh, she was very much a part of the Art Nouveau movement. Her style is often attributed to the influence of Aubrey Beardsley, but the delicacy of her line and colour was very much the product of her own imaginative world, populated as it was by her real belief in fairies. In 1902 she won a gold medal for her drawings at the Turin International Exhibition of Modern Decorative Art. Her illustrated books include William Morris's The Defence of Queen Guinevere and Other Poems *(1906), Milton's* Comus *(1906) and Oscar Wilde's* A House of Pomegranates *(1915), after which there was a noticeable strengthening in her use of both line and colour. She also illustrated for a number of magazines, including* The Studio.

1 *BOOK:* PONTS DE PARIS

DATE: 1912

2 *BOOK:* THE STUDIO

DATE: 1919

JESSIE WILCOX SMITH (1863–1935)

Born in Philadelphia, USA. Studied at the Pennsylvania Academy of Fine Art under Thomas Eakins, and at the Drexel Institute under Howard Pyle. Abandoning her original plans to be a kindergarten teacher, she concentrated instead on a career as an illustrator. She became very successful, especially with her portrayals of mothers and babies and children at work and at play, and illustrated a number of books, including Robert Louis Stevenson's A Child's Garden of Verses *(1905), Charles Kingsley's* The Water Babies *(1911), Johanna Spyri's* Heidi *(1922), a US edition of* Alice in Wonderland *and Louisa M Alcott's* Little Women *(1915). She also worked for a number of advertising clients, and contributed to* Ladies' Home Journal, Collier's, Harper's, Scribner's *and* The Century. *From 1918 to 1932 her pictures of adorable, beautifully dressed children appeared monthly on the covers of* Good Housekeeping *magazine.*

1—3 *BOOK:* MOTHER GOOSE

DATE: 1914

4 *BOOK:* THE WATER BABIES
by Charles Kingsley

DATE: 1911

5 *BOOK:*
THE EVERYDAY FAIRY BOOK

DATE: 1917

1

2

3

4

5

1

SIR WILLIAM RUSSELL FLINT
(1880–1969)

*Born in Edinburgh, Scotland. Trained at
Heatherley's Art School in London and
subsequently joined the staff of* The
Illustrated London News, *where he
remained until 1907. Books illustrated include*
The Song of Solomon *(1909),* The
Imitation of Christ *(1908), Joseph Conrad's*
The Duel *(1905), Chaucer's* The
Canterbury Tales *(1913) and Malory's* Le
Morte D'Arthur *(1911). Magazine clients
included* Tatler, The English Illustrated
Magazine, Black & White, The Idler *and*
The Sketch. *From the 1920s, Flint made his
name as a technically brilliant watercolourist,
specializing in scenes featuring sensual semi-
nude nymphets in idealized landscapes. These,
and his colour illustrations for lavishly
produced gift books, published by the Medici
Society, were enthusiastically acclaimed by the
public. He was elected Royal Academician in
1933 and was knighted in 1947.*

1 *BOOK:* LE MORTE D'ARTHUR
by Thomas Malory

DATE: 1911

2 *BOOK:* THE HEROES
by Charles Kingsley

DATE: 1912

2

JAMES MONTGOMERY FLAGG
(1877–1960)

Born in New York. He started drawing as a child and by the age of 14 was already financially independent of his family through selling his drawings. At 14 he sold his first illustration to Life *magazine, and subsequently became a member of its staff. At 16 he studied at the Art Students League in New York and at 20 he spent a year in England, where he illustrated his first book,* Yankee Girls Abroad. *Magazine clients included* Judge, Life, Good Housekeeping, Cosmopolitan, Liberty *and* Harper's Weekly. *From 1903 he drew portraits of the Hollywood stars for* Photoplay *magazine and these were later collated in a book called* Celebrities *(1951). Other books include* City People *(1909) and* The Adventures of Kitty Cobb *(1912). Flagg designed 46 posters for the war effort during World War I, including the "I Want You" image for* Leslie's Weekly. *During World War II, his "Uncle Sam" posters re-emerged and could be found outside recruiting stations across America.*

1	*POSTER:* U.S. MARINES
	DATE: c. 1914
2	*POSTER:* U.S. ARMY
	DATE: c. 1914
3	*MAGAZINE:* COSMOPOLITAN
	DATE: 1918
4	*MAGAZINE:* COSMOPOLITAN
	DATE: 1918

V L DANVERS (fl. 1920–1940)

Illustrator, graphic designer and poster designer. His work tended to rely on strong, simple imagery and flat colours, and was perfectly suited to the style that emerged from the development of the London Underground and LNER railway posters in the 1930s. In 1926 he wrote and illustrated a book, Training in Commercial Art, *which covered every aspect of the subject. In his instructions on the subject of travel posters he reveals the underlying principles of his own work: "It is not easy to render trees, grass-lands, water etc. in broad flat treatment. Make careful studies of the different formations and shapes of trees, shrubs etc. Whenever possible avoid putting in clouds. Clear skies indicate fine weather and clear atmosphere." His work was prolific and he was a champion of the belief that the aesthetic statements of commercial art were as important and as valid as those found in fine art.*

1 *ADVERTISEMENT:* SHELL	
DATE: 1926	
2 *POSTER:* LNER	
DATE: 1920	
3 *POSTER:* LNER	
DATE: 1924	

1

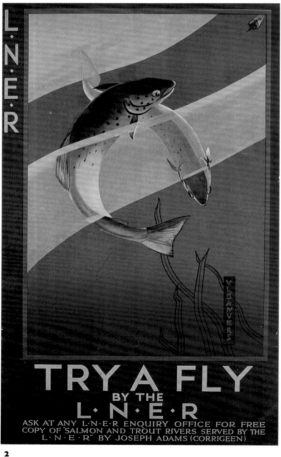

2

3

1

2

3

4

MAXWELL ARMFIELD (1882–1972)

Born in Ringwood, UK. Studied at Birmingham School of Art and in France and Italy. He lived in the USA between 1915 and 1922, and lectured on design and stage decoration at the Universities of Columbia, California and New Mexico, and published a number of books on technique. He was also a painter, etcher, poet, composer and writer.

Books illustrated include his own The Hanging Garden *(1914), Andersen's* The Ugly Duckling and Other Tales *(1913), Armfield's Animal Book (1922) and Shakespeare's* The Winter's Tale. *Armfield was a leading member of the Tempera Society, and his decorative works, executed with care and refinement, were influenced by early Renaissance painting.*

1, 2 *BOOK:*
ARMFIELD'S ANIMAL BOOK

DATE: 1922

3, 4 *BOOK:*
HANS ANDERSEN'S TALES

DATE: 1910

LEONETTO CAPIELLO (1875–1942)

Born at Livorno, Italy. After studies in his native town, he settled in Paris to work as a poster artist and illustrator. He published a book of caricatures (1896) and contributed to Le Rive, Le Journal, Le Figaro *and* Le Gaulois. *His theatre and advertising posters — such as "Folies-Bergère" (1900), "Cinzano" (1910) and "Le P'tit Jeune Homme" (for the play "Polaire", 1910) — show his mastery of line and rhythm, and he held to the importance of these elements, believing colour to be a secondary factor in the success of a design. In reducing the graphic elaboration that had been a feature of earlier poster work, Capiello moved towards the modern interpretation of the poster as an instantly attractive and memorable image.*

1 *ADVERTISEMENT:*
REVEL UMBRELLAS

DATE: 1922

2 *ADVERTISEMENT:*
THERMOGÈNE

DATE: 1909

3 *ADVERTISEMENT:*
CAMPARI CORDIAL

DATE: 1921

1

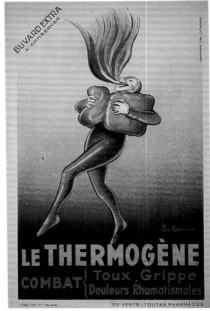

2

3

HARRY CLARKE (1889–1931)

Born in Dublin, Ireland, the son of a stained glass artist. Studied at Dublin Metropolitan School of Art, where he won a travelling scholarship in 1914 to study early stained glass in the Ile-de-France. Clarke was one of the most successful followers of Beardsley, his imagery encompassing a powerful blend of horror, drama and humour. He is remembered today both for the beauty of his illustrations for the fairy tales of Hans Andersen and Charles Perrault and for the power and invention of his horror-fantasy style, which has influenced many fantasy and science fiction artists since. His illustrations for Edgar Allan Poe's Tales of Mystery and Imagination *(1919) and Goethe's* Faust *(1925) moved an art critic, writing in* The Studio *in 1923, to write: "Never before have these marvellous tales been visually interpreted with such flesh-creeping, brain-taunting illusions of horror, terror and the unspeakable." Clarke was also a talented designer of stained glass and won the only gold medals awarded for stained glass at the Kensington Exhibitions in 1911, 1912 and 1913. He died of tuberculosis at the age of 42.*

I *BOOK:*
THE YEARS AT THE SPRING

DATE: 1920

2, 3 *BOOK:*
TALES OF MYSTERY AND
IMAGINATION
by Edgar Allan Poe

DATE: 1919

1

2

3

4

5

6

JOHN HASSALL (1868–1948)

Born in Walmer, UK, and educated in Devon and Heidelberg, Germany. After a brief spell as a farmer in Manitoba, Canada, he took up art, and had drawings accepted by The Graphic *and* Punch. *After studying art in Antwerp and Paris, he returned to England in 1895, where he became a successful cartoonist and advertising artist, designing some of the most effective posters of his day, including the well-known "Skegness Is So Bracing" (1908). He was granted a civil pension by George VI for his services to poster art. Hassall began illustrating children's books in the late 1890s, using the bold outlines and flat colour washes that characterized his posters. He also illustrated* John Hassall's New Picture Book *(1908),* Keep Smiling *(1916) and* Ye Berlyn Tapestrie *(1916), and contributed to* The Daily Sketch, Illustrated Bits, The Graphic, The Idler *and* The West End Review. *He was Principal of the London School of Art until it closed down in 1928.*

1 *POSTER:*
THE ARRIVAL OF PETER PAN

DATE: c. 1920

2 *TRAVEL POSTER:*
NORTH AFRICAN MOTOR TOURS

DATE: c. 1922

3 *ADVERTISEMENT:*
BOVRIL CHOCOLATE

DATE: c. 1920

4 *ADVERTISEMENT:*
EASTMAN'S CLEANING

DATE: c. 1900

5 *ADVERTISEMENT:*
HMV GRAMOPHONES

DATE: c. 1915

6 *BOOK:*
NURSERY RHYMES ILLUSTRATED

DATE: c. 1910

OTTO BAUMBERGER (1889–1961)

Born in Zurich, Switzerland. Apprenticed to a lithographer, then went on to study at the Konigliche Akademie in Munich, and also in Paris and London. In 1920 he worked on stage designs for productions in Berlin and Zurich, and in the same year began to teach lithography and life drawing at the School of Arts and Crafts in Zurich. Commercial work of the 1920s typically included "super-real" lithography images advertising clothing products — coats, hats, shoes — but he also produced highly graphic information posters constructed of geometric shapes and typography. During the 1930s he developed a looser, almost painterly style. His career demonstrated a range of design interests, from illustration and advertising design to stage design and mural painting.

1 *ADVERTISEMENT:* PKZ

DATE: 1922

2 *ADVERTISEMENT:*
FACO FLOOR COVERINGS

DATE: c. 1919

3 *ADVERTISEMENT:*
DOSENBACH'S SHOE MARKET

DATE: c. 1919

4 *ADVERTISEMENT:*
WECK

DATE: c. 1919

1

2

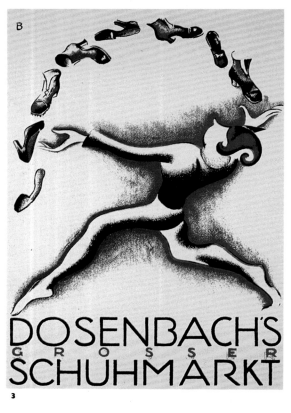

3

4

1

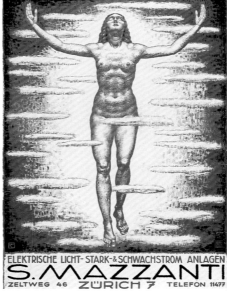

2

3

KARL BICKEL (1886—1949)

*Born in Zurich. During his lifetime Bickel
worked as an illustrator, painter, sculptor and
graphic artist. From 1900-04 he was an
apprentice lithographer and then spent four
years in a Zurich advertising agency while
taking evening classes at the School of Arts and
Crafts, where he studied under E Stiefel. In
1908 he started his own advertising agency
and continued his studies until he moved to
Italy in 1912. He spent a year there and was
strongly influenced by the works of
Michelangelo and Leonardo da Vinci. On his
return to Switzerland he made his first
attempts at sculpture and from 1914-17
concentrated on portraiture, etching and
landscape painting. From 1917 until his death
he was primarily a commercial artist,
designing and illustrating stamps, posters and
murals.*

1 *ADVERTISEMENT:*
SCHEURER SHOES

DATE: 1920

2 *ADVERTISEMENT:*
MAZZANTI LIGHTING

DATE: 1915

3 *TRAVEL POSTER:* AROSA

DATE: 1927

JEAN DE BOSSCHERE (1878–1953)

Born in Uccle, Belgium. Studied at the Beaux
Arts d'Anvers. After working in Paris,
Brussels, London and Italy, he finally settled
at Fontainebleau, near Paris, in 1929 (he
became a French citizen in 1959). His work
was wide-ranging, as writer, illustrator,
designer, printer and book collector. His first
book as author and illustrator was Béale-
Gyne *(1909): his own books included* The
City Curious *(1920) and* Job le Pauvre
(1923), and Gulliver's Travels *(1920) and*
Don Quixote *(1922) were among the classic*
titles that he illustrated. He also contributed to
The Little Review, The Monthly
Chapbook, The New Coterie, *and*
Reveille. *In his Beardsleyesque images, with*
solid blacks set against rhythmic lines, the
characterization sometimes has a hint of the
surreal.

1, 2 *BOOK:*
THE POEMS OF OSCAR WILDE

DATE: 1927

3, 4 *BOOK:* THE CITY CURIOUS

DATE: 1920

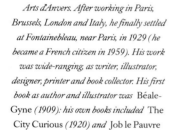

3

JOSEPH CHRISTIAN
LEYENDECKER (1874–1951)

*Born in Montabour, Germany. In 1882 he
moved with his parents to Chicago, USA, and
at age 16 was apprenticed to an engraving
company, at the same time taking evening
classes at the Chicago Art Institute. In 1896 he
won first prize in* The Century *magazine's
competition to illustrate one of their covers
(Maxfield Parrish came second) and he and
his younger brother studied at the Académie
Julien in Paris for two years before returning
to the USA to set up their own studio. His
illustrations appeared in magazines such as*
Collier's, Success, Up to Date *and* The
Saturday Evening Post. *He also illustrated
war bond posters (during World War II) and
advertisements for Kellogg's cornflakes, Ivory
soap, Chesterfield cigarettes and Arrow collars
and shirts. He originated the Arrow Shirt
collar man, which became the epitome of
elegant style sought after by the public.*

1 *MAGAZINE:*
THE SATURDAY EVENING POST

DATE: PUBLISHED 1940

2 *ADVERTISEMENT:*
ARROW COLLARS

DATE: 1913

3 *POSTER*

DATE: c. 1916

117

1

2

3

4

5

6

MABEL LUCIE ATTWELL
(1879–1964)

Born in London. Studied at the Regent Street and Heatherley Art Schools. From 1911 until the end of her life, Attwell's work appeared in annuals and gift books and on countless advertisements, posters, calendars, wall plaques and greetings cards, which she designed for Valentine of Dundee. Her chubby, mischievous toddlers, often featured in situations with adult overtones, conveyed a sentimental and nostalgic view of daily life between the wars. During the first decades of the century Attwell illustrated such fairy-tale classics as Mother Goose *(1910),* Alice in Wonderland *(1911) and* Hans Andersen's Fairy Tales *(1914), as well as Charles Kingsley's* The Water Babies *(1915) and J M Barrie's* Peter Pan and Wendy *(1921). She also contributed to* The Tatler, The Bystander, Graphic *and* The Illustrated London News.

1, 5, 6 *BOOK:*
PETER PAN AND WENDY
by J M Barrie

DATE: 1921

2 *GREETINGS CARD:*

DATE: c. 1920

3 *ADVERTISEMENT:*
VIM CLEANING POWDER

DATE: c. 1910

4 *POSTER:*
"WHERE DO FLIES GO IN WINTER-TIME?"

DATE: c. 1915

ROBERT GIBBINGS (1889–1958)

Born in Cork, Ireland. His parents wanted him to be a doctor but, after failing at medical school, he was eventually allowed to attend the Slade School of Art in London. His career was then stalled by World War I, during which he served at Gallipoli, and it was not until 1918 that he became a freelance artist, specializing in wood engraving. His early work tended to the simplicity of silhouettes, but in time he developed an extraordinarily precise technique that brought a great richness of detail to his engravings. In 1924 he bought the Golden Cockerel Press and set up as a printer of fine editions. He sold it in 1933 and lectured on book production at Reading University until 1942, when he left to concentrate on his own work and to travel. In all, he illustrated 61 books and was the author of 14, including Lovely is the Lee *(1945),* Coming Down the Wye *(1952),* Sweet Cork of Thee *(1951).* Coming Down the Seine *(1953) and* Trumpets from Montparnasse *(1955). His last work,* Till I End My Song, *was published in 1957, a year before his death.*

1 *BOOK:*
THE GIRL IN THE GARRET
by Robert Gibbings

DATE: 1921

2 *POSTER:* LONDON TRANSPORT

DATE: 1922

3 *WOOD ENGRAVING:*
"FOWEY HARBOUR"

DATE: 1921

4 *WOOD ENGRAVING:*
"CHELSEA BRIDGE"

DATE: 1921

1

2

CARL MOOS (1878–1959)

Born in Munich, Germany, son of the portrait painter Franz Moos. In 1897 he began his career as an illustrator for a Munich daily newspaper. In 1915 he established himself in Munich, where he divided his time between painting mountain landscapes and working for a local design group. His excellent draughtsmanship, combined with gentle but graphic use of colour, ensured his success both as an illustrator of posters and as a scenic artist.

1 *POSTER:*
"VOTE FOR FREEDOM OF THE SPIRIT"

DATE: 1935

2 *ADVERTISEMENT:* CAFFÈ HAG

DATE: 1927

3 *TRAVEL POSTER:* ST MORITZ

DATE: 1929

3

1

2

GEORGE E STUDDY
(1878–1948)

Born in Devon, UK. Studdy developed a childhood interest in drawing while confined to a hospital bed and later contributed his work to boys' magazines while a student at Dulwich College. On graduating from Heatherley's School of Art he worked as an engineer's draughtsman until 1906, when, after seeing the Royal Academy Summer Show, he was inspired to become a humorous artist. He illustrated regularly for The Sketch *magazine, where he developed the character of "Bonzo", the mischievous puppy which made him famous and which appeared on postcards, jigsaw puzzles and posters. In fact Bonzo became so popular that he escaped the confines of the media normally available to illustrators and appeared on ashtrays, car mascots, sweets, cigarette cards and other ephemera, all of which have become collectable items today. He also appeared in books and annuals and became a star of stage and screen. This craze peaked in the 1920s and Bonzo's popularity declined after Studdy's death from lung cancer in 1948.*

1, 2 *BOOK:* A BOX OF TRICKS

DATE: 1922

3, 4 *BOOK:* PUPPY TAILS

DATE: 1922

3

4

HARRY THEAKER (1873–1954)

Born in Wolstanton, UK. Studied at Burslem School of Art, the Royal College of Art, and in Italy. The range of his work included painting, book illustration and ceramic and stained glass design. From 1935-38 he held the post of Principal at the Regent Street Polytechnic School of Art in London. As an illustrator he is known for work on children's books, such as Charles Kingsley's The Water Babies *(1922),* Stories of King Arthur *(1925) and* Grimm's Fairy Tales *(1930), and he contributed to the periodical* Holly Leaves. *His skill as a watercolourist is reflected in the pleasing colouring of his illustrative work.*

1, 2 *BOOK:*
GULLIVER'S TRAVELS
by Jonathan Swift

DATE: 1920

3 *BOOK:* GRIMM'S FAIRY TALES

DATE: 1930

1

2

3

"Goodbye, Sweetheart, Goodbye.

1

Pre-historic Courtship.

Nº 3 "MARRIAGE".

2

3

4

5

LAWSON WOOD (1878–1957)

Born in London. Studied at Heatherley's and the Slade Art Schools and at Frank Calderon's School of Animal Painting. From 1896-1902 he was chief artist at the magazine publishers Arthur Pearson Ltd, during which time he gained valuable practical experience in commercial work and learned about the printing process so that he could best ensure the quality of his published drawings. During his career he became very popular with the public for his witty and technically brilliant illustrations of animals and people and contributed to Graphic, The Illustrated London News *and* Punch. *He also illustrated a number of books, including* Old Nursery Rhymes *(1931),* Lawson Wood's Fun Fair *(1931) and his famous series* The Merry Monkeys *(1946). He was a close friend of Tom Browne and a fellow member of the London Sketch Club.*

1 POSTCARD
DATE: 1906

2 POSTCARD
DATE: 1906

3, 4 *BOOK:* THE MERRY MONKEYS *by Arthur Groom*
DATE: 1946

5 *BOOK:* BRUSH, PEN AND PENCIL *by A E Johnson*
DATE: 1910

FRED TAYLOR (1875–1963)

Born in London. Studied at the Académie Julien in Paris, Goldsmith's College School of Art in London, and in Italy. An accomplished landscape and architectural painter, he was one of the artists commissioned for poster work by London Midland & Scottish Railways and London Underground during the 1920s and 1930s. Images such as "The Heart of the Empire", an aerial view of Westminster and the Houses of Parliament, "Trafalgar Square", and "Chigwell", a graphic view of a Tudor-style inn, show Taylor's superb grasp of architectural structure and detail and a subtle approach to colour, while "Hampstead Fair" describes the holiday crowd enjoying the fair in a riot of bold, bright hues. His control of line in black-and-white rendering is equally crisp and immediate.

1 *POSTER:* ENSIGNETTE
DATE: c. 1915

2 *POSTER:*
LONDON UNDERGROUND
DATE: 1920

3 *POSTER:*
LONDON & NORTH EASTERN
RAILWAY
DATE: c. 1923

1

2

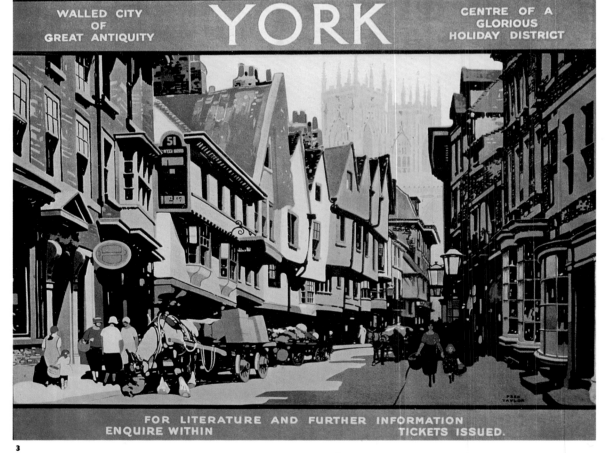

3

1

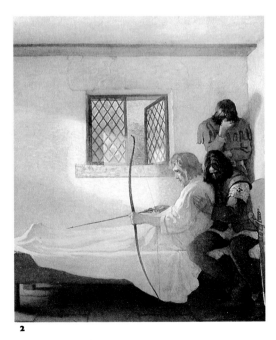

2

3

NEWELL CONVERS WYETH
(1882–1945)

Born in Needham, USA. Wyeth was a devotee of his teacher, Howard Pyle, and depicted similar subjects — medieval life, Americana and pirates — and captured dramatic scenes in rich decorative colours. He was extremely prolific and during his lifetime produced more than 3,000 illustrations, murals, still lifes and landscape paintings. Among them were more than 25 books for Charles Scribner's Sons' Classic Series, *including J Boyd's* Drums *(1928), Stevenson's* David Balfour *(1924) and J F Cooper's* The Deerslayer *(1925), some of which are still in print today. One of the finest examples of his work is J F Cooper's* Last of the Mohicans *(1919). He was an extremely popular figure in America, and his skills were inherited by his extraordinarily talented family — most notable being his son Andrew.*

1, 2 *BOOK:* ROBIN HOOD

DATE: 1921

3 *PAINTING:*
"INDIAN BRAVE FISHING"

DATE: c. 1900

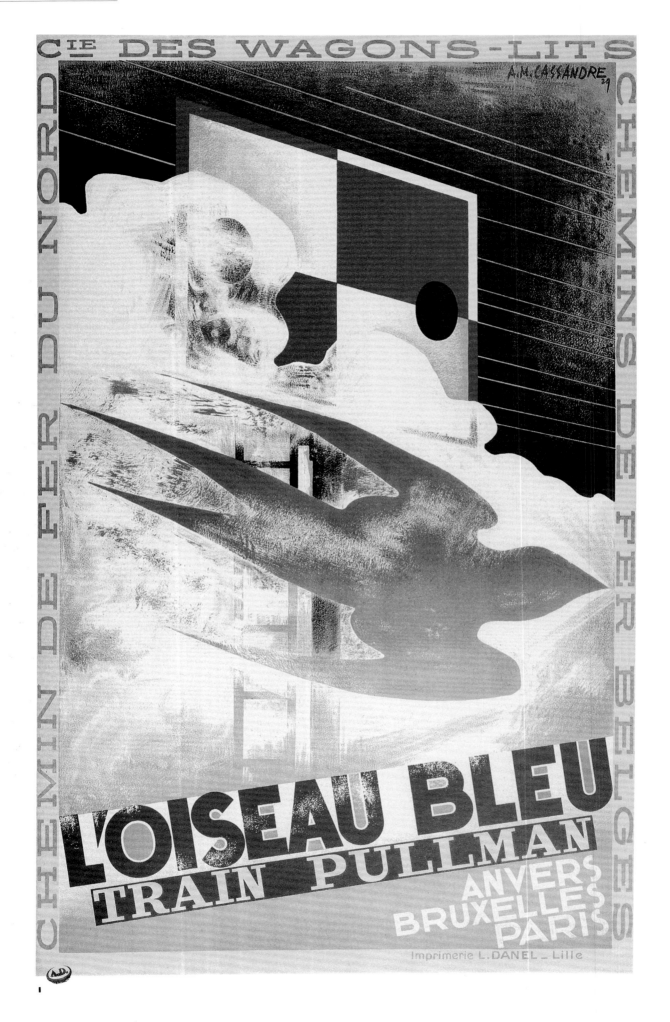

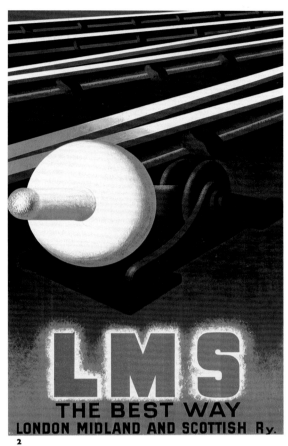

2

3

4

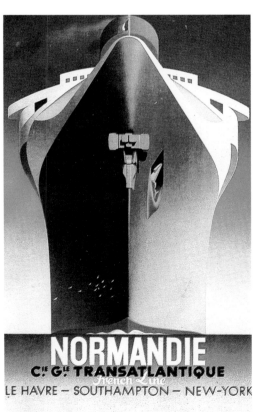

5

A M CASSANDRE (1901–1968)

Born Adolphe Mouran in Russia. Studied at the Académie Julien in Paris. From 1922-28 he designed posters for Hachard and Co, and in 1930 he founded the Alliance Graphique with Charles Loupot and Maurice Moyrand. Influenced by Léger, Delaunay and the Italian Futurists, he took elements from avant-garde painting and design and popularized them in his brilliant posters, widely acknowledged as among the best to have come out of France during the 1930s. His designs for the French National Railways, and those for the ocean liners L'Atlantique (1931) and Normandie (1935), are classics of their genre. He also designed theatre sets and costumes, typefaces for Olivetti, and ran a small art school, where André François was one of his pupils.

1 *POSTER:* BELGIAN RAILWAYS

DATE: 1929

2 *POSTER:*
LONDON, MIDLAND & SCOTTISH RAILWAY

DATE: 1928

3 *POSTER:*
FRENCH NORTHERN RAILWAYS

DATE: 1929

4 *POSTER:* BELGIAN RAILWAYS

DATE: 1927

5 *POSTER:*
FRENCH TRANSATLANTIC LINE

DATE: 1935

1

WILLY POGANY (1882–1955)

Born in Szeged, Hungary. He started working while still a child, to help support his family after his father's death, and paid for his own education at the Budapest Technical School, where he studied engineering, by giving tuition to fellow students. He later attended the Academy of Art in Budapest and studied art in Paris and Munich. In 1906 he moved to London, where he became a protégé of Edmund Dulac (a fellow member of the London Sketch Club) and where he became a very successful illustrator. Books illustrated include The Rime of the Ancient Mariner *(1910),* The Rubaiyat of Omar Khayyam *(1909) and Goethe's* Faust *(1912). In 1915 he settled in New York, where he continued to illustrate books and also designed hotel interiors and stage sets. He worked in Hollywood as an art director for Warner Studios until the 1930s. Pogány's best illustrations were in pen and ink, a medium in which he was remarkably fluent.*

1 *MAGAZINE:*
LE JOURNAL DE LA DECORATION

DATE: c. 1900

2 ORIENTAL MOTIFS NO 4

DATE: c. 1900

3 ORIENTAL MOTIFS NO 3

DATE: c. 1900

4 *BOOK:*
LEGENDS OF THE MIDDLE AGES

DATE: 1914

5, 6 *BOOK:* NURSERY RHYMES

DATE: 1919

7 *BOOK:* GULLIVER'S TRAVELS
by Jonathan Swift

DATE: 1919

2   3

4

5

6

7

EDMUND SULLIVAN (1869–1933)

*Born in London. His father was an artist and
Sullivan studied under him until the age of 20,
when he joined The Daily Graphic.
Although perhaps overshadowed by Dulac
and Rackham, he quickly established himself
as a fine draughtsman with two distinct styles
— black-and-white work in pen and ink and a
looser, gentler treatment with washes and
chalk lines. He was a devotee of Phil May and,
in his own words, wanted to express "the
character the solid body is possessed of — the
spiritual essence . . . and the impact made on
the whole complex mind and not only upon, or
by, the retina". He contributed to many of the
publications of his day and illustrated nearly
20 books, including Wells'* Modern Utopia
(1905), The Pilgrim's Progress *(1901) and*
The Rubaiyat of Omar Khayyam *(1913).
He was also highly influential as a teacher,
lecturing at Goldsmith's College of Art and
producing a detailed instruction manual,* The
Art of Illustration *(1921).*

1 *BOOK:*
DREAM OF FAIR WOMEN
by Alfred Tennyson

DATE: 1900

2 *ADVERTISEMENT:* SHELL FUELS

DATE: 1923

1

2

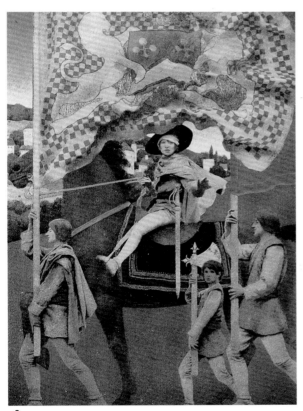

MAXFIELD PARRISH (1870–1966)

*Born in Philadelphia, USA. Educated at
Haverford College, the Pennsylvania Academy
of Fine Arts, and studied under Howard Pyle
at the Drexel Institute. He illustrated for a
number of magazines, including* Harper's
Weekly, Collier's *and* Time. *Books
illustrated include* Dream Days *(1906) by
Kenneth Grahame,* Poems of Childhood
(1889) by Eugene Field and The Knave of
Hearts *(1925) by Louise Saunders. His
unique combination of colour, exotic characters
and fanciful settings won him much popular
acclaim during his lifetime.*

1 *ADVERTISEMENT:* JELL-O DESSERT
DATE: 1924

2 *BOOK:* THE KING ALBERT BOOK
DATE: 1914

3 *MAGAZINE:* THE CENTURY
DATE: c. 1930

ERIC GILL (1882–1940)

Born in Brighton, UK. Studied at Chichester Art School and the Central School of Arts and Crafts in London. He began his career as a letter-cutter and sign writer, then turned to figure carving in wood and stone. In 1913 he became a Catholic and, after World War I, formed the Guild of St Joseph and St Dominic — a society of craftsmen dedicated to reviving a religious attitude towards art and craft. A versatile artist, he was a very skilful engraver, illustrating many books for Robert Gibbings at the Golden Cockerel Press from 1924. He was also a sculptor of international repute and played an enormous part in the development of English 20th-century typography.

I *BOOK:* THE FOUR GOSPELS

DATE: 1931

2 *BOOK:*
PASSIO DOMINI NOSTRI
JESU CHRISTI

DATE: 1926

3 *BOOK JACKET:*
THE ALDINE BIBLE

DATE: 1934

DUDLEY HARDY (1867–1922)

Born in Sheffield, UK. Studied at the Academy of Art in Dusseldorf, where he was a rebellious student, and was expelled in 1884. He returned to England before continuing his studies in Antwerp and Paris, where French poster art had a lasting influence on his own work. His most famous posters are "The Gaiety Girl", for Sir Augustus Harris's theatrical venture, and "The Yellow Girl", which advertised Jerome K Jerome's new publication Today. *The latter was particularly popular and started a craze for posters in England.*

I *PROGRAMME DESIGN:*
BERTRAM MILLS' CIRCUS

DATE: 1921

I

2

3

CHARLES PAINE (1873–1964)

Born in Queenstown, Pennsylvania, USA. In 1886 he drew cartoons for the Pittsburgh Post, *using the trademark of a little racoon. Over the next few years he created other strips, including* Coon Hollow Folks, Bear Creek Folks *and* Scary William, *for newspapers in Pittsburgh and Philadelphia. Paine had a very individual and decorative style, with sketchy, boldly coloured figures drawn inside circles, rather than the usual panel format. When he became successful he moved to California, from where he sent* Honeybunch's Hubby *to New York for publication three times a week. However, his fame rests on his classic strip* S'Matter Pop? *featuring the adventures of Pop, Willyum and Desperate Ambrose. It was first published in* World *in 1917 and ran for 30 years. After its demise, Paine fell into obscurity and died penniless in New York.*

1 *ADVERTISEMENT:* SHELL OIL

DATE: 1928

2 *POSTER:* LONDON TRANSPORT

DATE: 1922

3 *PUBLICITY POSTER:* WELWYN GARDEN CITY

DATE: 1939

1

2

KATHE KOLLWITZ (1867–1945)

Born Käthe Schmidt in Konigsberg, Germany. Studied painting in Munich, where she discovered what was to become a life-long preference for black-and-white media. She married a doctor and lived in the poor northern sector of Berlin, where her husband worked and where she took up etching. Sharing with Gauguin the belief that "ugliness can be beautiful, prettiness never", her art was an expression of her solidarity with the oppressed and poverty-stricken. In the late 1890s she achieved fame as a socialist artist with her illustrations for Hauptmann's The Weavers' Uprising, *and in 1902 she was much praised for her series* The Peasants' War, *In 1909 she contributed drawings to the satirical magazine* Simplizissimus *and the following year took up sculpture. In 1919 she began producing woodcuts, a medium whose bold simplicity was well suited to her subjects and themes. Her son was killed in World War I and she remained passionately opposed to war, producing "The War" series of woodcuts in 1923.*

1 *ETCHING:* "PEASANTS' WAR"

DATE: 1903

2 *ETCHING:* "PEASANTS' WAR"

DATE: 1907

EDWARD PENFIELD (1866—1925)

Illustrator, poster artist and writer, born in the USA. While Lautrec, Mucha and Chéret were enjoying the "Golden Age of the Poster" in Europe, Penfield was producing some of the best poster work in America. His style was to draw in silhouetted shapes that had been refined from careful preliminary sketches. The effect was deceptive, in that when seen from a distance the simplicity of the treatment made the subject immediately recognizable and yet when seen in close-up the work contained sufficient detail to hold the viewer's interest. In the first two decades of the century his work appeared frequently on the covers of magazines such as Collier's *and he illustrated many calendars, the most notable being his redrawing of the* Old Farmer's Almanac *for the Beck Engraving Company in 1918. He also wrote and illustrated the outstanding* Holland Sketches, *which was published by Scribner's in 1907. Penfield had a lasting influence on American illustration through his work, his teaching at the Art Students League and his years as art director of* Harper's *magazine. He was president of the Society of Illustrators in 1921 and 1922.*

1 *BOOK:*
THREE GRINGOS IN CENTRAL AMERICA AND VENEZUELA
by Richard Harding

DATE: c. 1900

2 *PUBLICITY POSTER:*
HARPER'S MAGAZINE

DATE: c. 1900

3 *ADVERTISEMENT:*
HART SCHAFFNER & MARX OUTFITTERS

DATE: NOT KNOWN

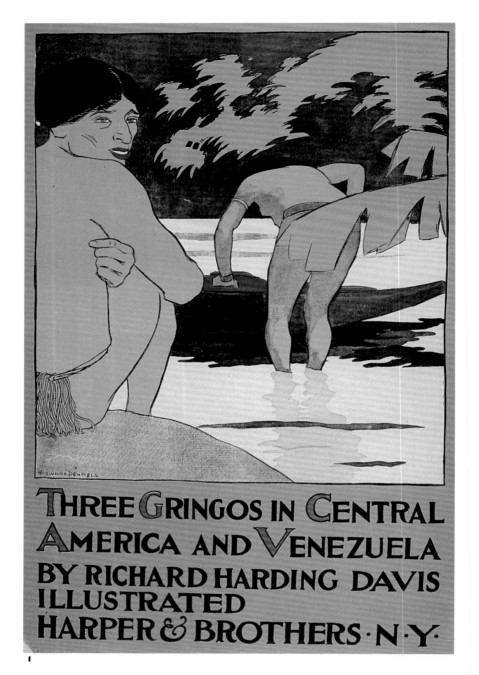

1

2

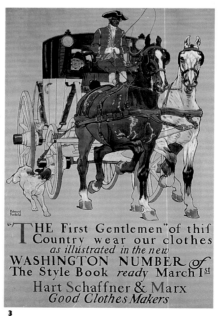

3

WILL OWEN (1869–1957)

Born in Malta. Studied at Lambeth School of Art. He developed a humorous style with heavy outlines that was reminiscent of his contemporaries, John Hassall and Tom Browne. His work was very popular and he contributed frequently to magazines such as Punch, The Sketch, Tatler, The Strand Magazine, The Graphic, The Idler *and* the Humorist. *He developed a working relationship with the humorous writer W W Jacobs and illustrated four of his books, including* Sailor's Knots *(1909) and* Short Cruises *(1920). He also wrote and illustrated five books of his own —* Alleged Humour *(1917),* Three Jolly Sailors and Me *(1919),* Old London Town *(1921),* Mr Peppercorn *(1940) and* What's The Dope? *(1944). However, his style was best suited to posters and he produced a great many for such clients as Lux washing powders and Sunlight soap.*

1	*ADVERTISEMENT:* LUX SOAP FLAKES
	DATE: c. 1920
2	*ADVERTISEMENT:* SUNLIGHT SOAP
	DATE: c. 1920
3	*PUBLICITY POSTER*
	DATE: c. 1920

HERBERT K. ROOKE

BURNHAM BEECHES

1

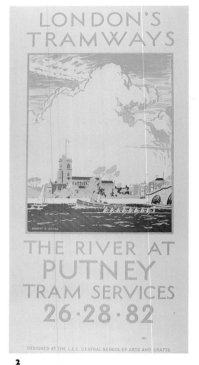

2

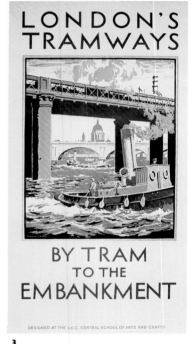

3

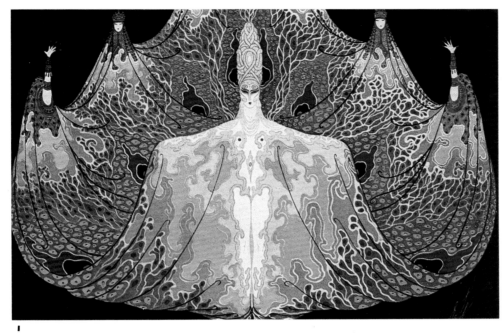

1

2

NOEL ROOKE (1881–1953)

Grew up and was schooled in France. The son of a portrait painter, Rooke studied at the Slade in London from 1899-1903 and then under Edward Johnstone at the Central School of Art, where Eric Gill was one of his contemporaries. In 1904 he took up wood engraving. He drew directly on to the wood block, working in both black and white line, and experimented with graduated tones and wood-cutting. Although he was familiar with the techniques of colour printing, he mostly limited himself to black and white in his book illustrations.

1	*POSTER:* LONDON TRANSPORT
	DATE: c. 1900
2	*POSTER:* LONDON TRAMWAYS
	DATE: c. 1900
3	*POSTER:* LONDON TRAMWAYS
	DATE: c. 1900

ERTE (b. 1892)

Born in St Petersburg (Leningrad), Russia. Moving to Paris in 1912, he became a designer with the couturier Paul Poiret. He adopted the pseudonym Erté from the French pronunciation of his initials, R T (Romain de Tirtoff). He designed magazine covers and fashion plates for Harper's Bazaar *over a period of more than 20 years, although he also contributed to* Vogue *and others. Erté's designs were typically elaborate and stylish. His illustrations, in black and white or vivid colour, ranged from richly decorative Art Deco fantasies to fluidly elegant, practical modern clothing, and he was frequently able to combine a graphic visual economy with careful attention to descriptive detail.*

1	*COSTUME DESIGN*
	DATE: c. 1920
2	*COSTUME DESIGN*
	DATE: 1921

1

2

GEORGE GROSZ (1893–1959)

*Born Georg Ehrenfried Groß in Germany.
Studied at the Dresden Academy of Art and
had his first satirical drawings published in
the comic magazine* Ulk *at the age of 17. He
also studied in Paris and at the Berlin School
of Arts and Crafts, where he made a living by
selling his caricatures. By 1919 he was a
leading member of the Dada art movement in
Berlin, and, with John Heartfield, edited
satirical magazines of the political left which
made him unpopular with the Nazis. An
opponent of what he called "the slavish
copying of nature", he believed in the
expressive use of line. At his most brilliant in
*Ecce Homo *(1923), which was confiscated
by the police and led to an indecency trial,
Grosz's harsh images and startling use of line
and colour perfectly express his contempt for
the decadent bourgeoisie. His illustrations have
had an enormous influence on subsequent
generations of artists and illustrators. In 1932
he moved to New York, where he taught at the
Art Students League.*

1–7 *BOOK:* ECCE HOMO

DATE: 1923

3

4

5

6

7

HARRISON FISHER (1875–1934)

Born in New York. His early talent for drawing was encouraged, and he studied at the Mark Hopkins Institute of Art in San Francisco. At the age of 16, and while still a student, his work was published in the local newspapers. After leaving college he returned to New York and worked as a staff artist on Puck. *By now his talent for drawing women was established; his Fisher Body Girl was a trademark for years and led to an exclusive contract to illustrate the monthly covers for* Cosmopolitan *magazine, which he did for several years.*

1 *MAGAZINE:* COSMOPOLITAN
DATE: 1920

2 *MAGAZINE:* COSMOPOLITAN
DATE: 1920

3 *MAGAZINE:* COSMOPOLITAN
DATE: 1920

4 *MAGAZINE:* COSMOPOLITAN
DATE: 1920

HOWARD CHANDLER CHRISTY
(1873–1952)

Born in Ohio, USA. Studied at the Art Students League and the National Academy in New York, and was taken on by William Merritt Chase as a private student at his famous 10th Street Studio. Initially Christy planned to be a fine artist, but after selling his work to Scribner's, Harper's *and* Leslie's Weekly *he chose a more commercial career. During the Spanish-American conflict he worked as a War Artist and went with the US troops to Cuba. However, he is remembered mostly for his drawings of women. His subjects were usually healthy, outdoor types who became known as the "Christy Girls", and were popular with the public and with magazine publishers.*

1 *MAGAZINE:* COSMOPOLITAN
DATE: 1918

Little Jack Horner sat in a corner,
Eating a Christmas pie

59

2

ANNE ANDERSON (1874–1930)

*Born in Scotland, but spent her childhood in
Argentina before finally settling in England.
She worked on over 100 children's books,
including treasuries and annuals, sometimes in
collaboration with her husband, Alan Wright.
She produced several titles as both author and
illustrator, among them* The Funny Bunny
ABC *(1912),* The Cosy Corner Book
(1943), and The Podgy Puppy *(1927). Her
decorative line work and delicate colouring
showed the influence of Art Nouveau and also
owed something to the style of Mabel Lucie
Attwell. Her illustrations were particularly
popular during the 1920s and she also
produced greetings card designs. Her work has
proved enduringly popular and her illustrated*
Grimm's Fairy Tales *(1928 and 1929) have
been reprinted many times.*

I *CHRISTMAS CARD*

DATE: c. 1930

2 *BOOK:*
OLD ENGLISH NURSERY SONGS

DATE: NOT KNOWN

3 *BOOK:*
THE GOLDEN WONDER BOOK

DATE: 1934

4 *BOOK:*
OLD ENGLISH NURSERY SONGS

DATE: NOT KNOWN

1

3

4

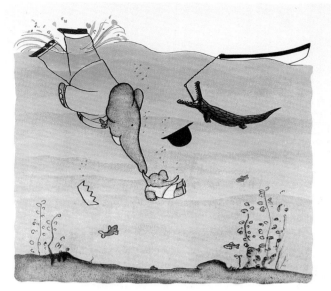

Like all little boys, Arthur and Zephir
were always up to mischief;
but they were not lazy.
At the old lady's house, Babar and Celeste
were astonished to hear them playing
the violin and 'cello.
"It's wonderful!" cried Celeste,
and Babar said:
"Children, I am pleased with you.
Go to the cake-shop and
choose whatever you like."

1

2

3

4

JEAN DE BRUNHOFF (1899–1937)

*Born in Paris. Studied under Othon Friesz.
De Brunhoff will always be remembered for
his stories and illustrations of Babar the
Elephant, a character he created for the
amusement of his children. The simple
watercolour drawings were accompanied by
text in clear but child-like handwriting. The
first book,* The Story of Babar, *was
published in Paris in 1931 and soon after in
London and New York, and was an
immediate success.* Babar's Travels *and*
Babar the King *soon followed, and the stories
of Babar and the inhabitants of the town of
Celesteville were serialized in* The Daily
Sketch *in the UK. In 1936 the books were
translated into eight languages, making Babar
the internationally famous character that he
remains to this day. De Brunhoff died at the
age of 38 and the last two books,* Babar and
Family *(1938) and* Babar and Father
Christmas *(1939), were completed by his
brother Michel and son Laurent. In 1988
Babar reached the big screen in* The Babar
Story, *an English-speaking animated feature
directed by Alan Bunce.*

1—3 *BOOK:*
BABAR THE KING
by Jean de Brunhoff

DATE: 1938

4 *BOOK:*
BABAR AND FATHER CHRISTMAS
by Jean de Brunhoff

DATE: c. 1939

HENRY MAYO BATEMAN
(1887–1970)

*Born in New South Wales, Australia. His
family returned to England when he was a
child and he studied at the Westminster and
New Cross Art Schools, after which he worked
in the studio of Charles Van Havenmaet for
several years. In 1906, encouraged by Phil
May (a fellow member of the London Sketch
Club), he began contributing humorous
drawings to* Tatler, Scraps, Punch *and* The
Graphic. *After 1911, he revolutionized
humorous art in Britain with his* The Man
Who ... *series of cartoons, which exploited
middle-class mores and the fear of committing
a faux pas. His barking colonels, haughty
matriarchs and timid little men were drawn
from his own social milieu, and the comic
situations focused on the social arenas of the
party, the club, and the meal table. Books
include* Bateman's Booklets *(1931),* The
Art of the Caricature *(1936) and* H M
Bateman by Himself *(1937). He also
illustrated advertisements for the London
tailors Moss Bros, Lucky Strike cigarettes and
Guinness beer, and designed theatre posters.*

1 *WWII POSTER:* "UP AND AT 'EM!"

DATE: c. 1939

2 *BOOK:* BROUGHT FORWARD

DATE: 1932

3 *ADVERTISEMENT:*
GUINNESS BEER

DATE: 1937

1

2

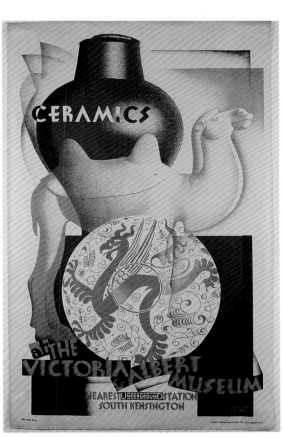

3

AUSTIN COOPER (1890–1964)

Born in Souris, Canada. His family moved to Wales in 1896 and he studied at art schools in Cardiff and Scotland, continuing evening studies after he moved to London to begin his career. After work in Canada as a commercial artist, interrupted by a period of service in Europe during World War I, he settled in London in 1922, where he developed a strong and colourful graphic style. Work for London Transport posters, such as his design for the Natural History Museum in London (1928), led to other similar commissions from the Royal Mail shipping company, BP Oil and many others. In 1943 he began to develop his painting skills independently of commercial work and became known as a painter of abstracts.

1 *ADVERTISEMENT:* BP OIL

DATE: 1933

2 *POSTER:* SOUTHERN RAILWAY

DATE: 1930

3 *POSTER:*
VICTORIA AND ALBERT MUSEUM

DATE: 1934

ROCKWELL KENT (1882–1971)

Born in New York. Trained as an architect but later studied art in New York with Robert Henri, Abbott Thayer and William Chase. He was one of a breed of American illustrators who combined artistic endeavour with a life of adventure. He spent the winter of 1918 on Fox Island in Alaska and his diaries and drawings were the source material for his own publication, Wilderness *(1920). This experience was still evident ten years later in his portrayal of* Moby Dick *(1930). However, neither work is really typical of his style. His architect's precision is better represented in* Salamina *(1935) and his interest in Art Deco in* Candide *(1928). His achievements went beyond illustration and he became famous as an engraver, lithographer, mural painter, writer and lecturer. Throughout his life he remained a controversial left-wing activist. He was blacklisted during the McCarthy era, in response to which he later refused the title of National Academician.*

1—3 *BOOK PLATES*

DATE: c. 1937

1

2

3

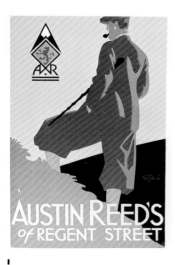

THE QUICK-STARTING PAIR. **SHELL OIL & PETROL**

1

2

3

4

TOM PURVIS (1889–1959)

Born in Bristol, UK. Studied at Camberwell School of Art and after graduating worked for six years in advertising before deciding to set up his own studio. He quickly became successful as a poster artist and from 1920-50 his prolific output could be seen on billboards and hoardings all over the UK. His style was characterized by the use of bold colours and minimal detail and his many clients included Dewar's whisky, Bovril, the LNER, Shell-Mex, BP and Austin Reed. In 1935 he helped organize the "British Art In Industry" exhibition at the Royal Academy and from 1940-45 he was an Official War Artist, attached to the Ministry of Supply, where he produced posters that boosted British morale and encouraged material economies.

1 *ADVERTISEMENT:* AUSTIN REED

DATE: c. 1930

2 *ADVERTISEMENT:* SHELL OIL

DATE: 1931

3 *ADVERTISEMENT:* SHELL OIL

DATE: 1930

4 *ADVERTISEMENT:* SHELL OIL

DATE: 1928

1

2

AUBREY HAMMOND (1894–1940)

Born in Folkestone, UK. Studied at the London and Byam Shaw Schools of Art, then attended the Académie Julien in Paris. He worked a great deal in pen and ink, drawing caricatures very much in the style of the 20s, and also developed a strong graphic style with flat colours that was extremely effective on posters. He illustrated several books, including The Diary of Mr Niggs *(1922), Lewis Melville's* The London Scene *(1926) and Peter Traill's* Under the Cherry Tree *(1926). He also worked as a scenic artist and taught commercial and theatrical design at the Westminster School of Art.*

1 *POSTER:*
LONDON TRANSPORT

DATE: 1923

2 *POSTCARD:*
CHARLES LAUGHTON

DATE: 1928

3 *ADVERTISEMENT:*
"232" GREY FLANNELS

DATE: c. 1928

3

Bathing Song

(*To the tune of "What are the Wild Waves Saying?"*)

" What are the wild waves saying,
                    Brother, the whole day long?
What is the tune they're playing—
                    Is it a popular song?"
"'Popular' just describes it,
                    And the message is also true,
For my medical man prescribes it—
                    Guinness is Good for You."

Farbige Anzeige für Guinness Bier   Entwurf und Agentur   S.H. BENSON Ltd.   Design and Agency   Coloured advertisement for Guinness

1

2

3

REX WHISTLER (1905–1944)

Born in Eltham, UK. He was an artistically gifted child and studied for a year at the Royal Academy Schools before enrolling at the Slade School of Fine Arts at the age of 17. Here he was encouraged by Professor Tonks and in 1926, when he was just 21, he was commissioned to paint a mural in the tea room at the Tate Gallery. Inspired by the Temple Gardens of Stowe and Wilton, Whistler created an architectural fantasy, called The Pursuit of Rare Meats, *that brought him immediate recognition and success. One of his earliest publications was* Children of Hertha *(1929), written by his brother Laurence. Whistler went on to illustrate three further books by his brother,* Armed October *(1932),* The Emperor Heart *(1936) and* Oho *(1946). However, his classic work is undoubtedly* Gulliver's Travels *(1930), which contained full-plate drawings in pen and ink with colour washes applied by hand. Whistler's work was always witty, and during the 1930s he produced a Guinness advertising campaign consisting of faces drawn in pen and ink which changed character when viewed upside down. He also designed for stage productions, including* The Rake's Progress, Victoria Regina, Fidelio *and* The Marriage of Figaro.

1 *ADVERTISEMENT:*
GUINNESS BEER

DATE: c. 1937

2 *BOOK:*
FAIRY TALES AND LEGENDS
by Hans Christian Andersen

DATE: 1935

3 *POSTER:* SHELL FUELS

DATE: 1933

153

OTTO ERNST (1884)

*Born in Kölliken, Switzerland. From 1906-07
he studied in Florence and Paris, where he
was a student of E Grasset at the Académie de
la Grande Chaumière. He then returned to
Switzerland, where he exhibited his
landscapes and lithographs and where his
graphic style made him a successful designer
and illustrator of posters.*

1 *POSTER:*
"WORLD CYCLE CHAMPIONSHIP"

DATE: 1923

2 *TRAVEL POSTER*

DATE: 1937

3 *TRAVEL POSTER*

DATE: 1930

1

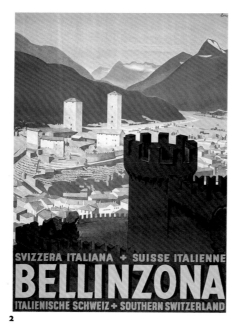

2

3

MARCELLO DUDOVICH
(1878–1962)

Born in Trieste, Italy. Educated in Bologna, where he later worked as a commercial artist. His mastery of line and use of strong colour and simple graphic designs made him a much sought after poster artist and he worked regularly for the Ricordi publishers in Milan and for advertising clients such as Gitane cigarettes in France. His work was exhibited in the Milan International Exhibition in 1905. He became a political caricaturist during the 1911 Tripoli War and was later a professor at the Brera Academy in Milan.

1	*ADVERTISING POSTER* SPIGA TYRES
DATE: 1931	
2	*POSTER*
DATE: c. 1925	
3	*POSTER*
DATE: c. 1920	
4	*ADVERTISING POSTER:* STREGA LIQUEUR
DATE: 1931	

GRAHAM SUTHERLAND
(1903–1980)

Born in London. Studied etching and engraving at Goldsmith's College of Art. In 1932 he took up painting, mainly semi-abstract landscapes of Wales, Cornwall and Pembrokeshire. An official War Artist during World War II, his illustrations of the devastation helped secure his developing reputation. From 1927-40 he taught at Kingston and Chelsea Schools of Art and designed stained glass and tableware decoration as well as illustrating for clients such as Jack Beddington at Shell. In 1942 he published his Pembrokeshire Sketchbook in Horizon *magazine. He remains most famous for his paintings, which were influenced by Samuel Palmer. In the late 1940s he began to concentrate on portraiture and painted Somerset Maugham in 1949 and Winston Churchill in 1954. This latter portrait caused a controversy and was later destroyed by Churchill's family. In 1956 he moved to the South of France and the following year received his most famous commission, the* Christ In Glory *Tapestry at Coventry Cathedral.*

1 *POSTER:* LONDON TRANSPORT
DATE: 1938

2 *POSTER:* LONDON TRANSPORT
DATE: 1935

3 *ADVERTISEMENT:* SHELL OIL
DATE: 1937

1

2

3

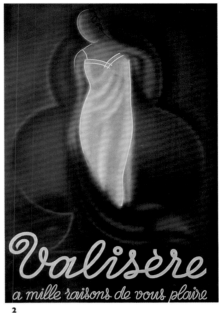

CHARLES LOUPOT (1892–1962)

Born in Nice, France. Trained at the Ecole des Beaux-Arts, Lyon. He first practised as a graphic artist in Switzerland before settling in Paris. From 1922 he was designing advertising materials for a number of French firms, including Voisin, Monsavon and Vichy-Celestin. Loupot's major contribution to a totally new approach to poster advertising came with the commission in 1938 to redesign the St Raphael-Quinquina poster. He devised a strongly graphic representation of the St Raphael name. Once established in the public eye, this was broken up into formal patterns and abstract designs which, though no longer displaying the full name, remained instantly identifiable with it. This work extended over almost 20 years, but Loupot's output was varied and extended into different styles and contexts. In 1931, he shared an exhibition of poster art with Cassandre and his work was included in exhibitions of advertising art worldwide. He contributed work to, among others, La Gazette du Bon Ton, Femina *and* Art et Industrie.

1 *ADVERTISEMENT:*
CAILLER CHOCOLATE

DATE: 1921

2 *ADVERTISEMENT:*
VALISÈRE LINGERIE

DATE: 1937

3 *ADVERTISEMENT:*
VALENTINE PRINT

DATE: 1929

1

2

ERNEST HOWARD SHEPARD
(1879–1976)

Born in London. Educated at St Paul's School, where his early talent for drawing was encouraged. He took extra classes at Heatherley's Art School and in 1897 won a scholarship to the Royal Academy Schools, where he was the Landseer scholar in 1899. He began drawing for Punch *in 1907, and in 1945 became their chief cartoonist, which he remained until he was sacked by Malcolm Muggeridge in 1953. He produced some impressive political cartoons during World War II, but his sensitive pen and ink style was more suited to childhood scenes and he is best remembered for his illustrations for A A Milne's* Winnie-the-Pooh *(1926) and Kenneth Grahame's* The Wind in the Willows *(1931).*

1, 2 *BOOK:*
THE WIND IN THE WILLOWS
by Kenneth Grahame

DATE: 1931

3 *BOOK:*
WHEN WE WERE VERY YOUNG
by A A Milne

DATE: 1924

4, 5 *BOOK:* WINNIE-THE-POOH
by A A Milne

DATE: 1926

3

4

5

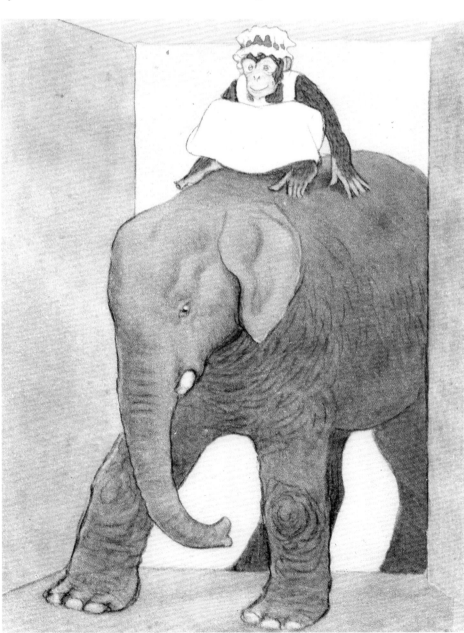

SUSAN B PEARSE (1878–1980)

*Born in Fair Oak, UK. Studied at New Cross
Art School and the Royal College of Art,
London. Married W E Webster, portrait
painter and illustrator. Her distinctive style of
children's book illustration shows a charmingly
decorative approach to form and composition
coupled with a sturdy sense of realistic detail.*

She illustrated several books, including
Dickens' Captain Boldheart *(1927), and
contributed to the periodical* Little Folks *and
to* Playbox Annual, *but is particularly
known for her series of* Ameliaranne *books,
in which her illustrations were provided with
texts by various writers, including Eleanor
Farjeon and M Gilmour. Her 1920 poster
illustration for Start-Rite shoes has become a
classic graphic image.*

1, 2 *BOOK:*
AMELIARANNE AT THE FARM
by M Gilmour

DATE: 1937

3 *BOOK:*
AMELIARANNE GIVES A CONCERT
by M Gilmour

DATE: PUBLISHED 1944

1

2

ZERO (1898—1976)

*Born Hans Schleger in Kempen, Germany.
Studied in Berlin and worked for five years in
the USA, initially as a freelance designer and
then as director of a New York advertising
agency, where he adopted the name "Zero"
when signing his work. In 1932 he moved to
London and became a British citizen in 1938.
He established his own studio and design
consultancy and his work covered the full
spectrum of graphic and commercial art. He
was influenced by the Bauhaus, A M
Cassandre and his close friend E McKnight
Kauffer. As well as designing posters for clients
such as Shell, MacFisheries, London
Transport and the Post Office, he pioneered the
concept of corporate identity in the UK,
illustrated book jackets, designed exhibitions
and packaging and created the symbol for
London bus stops and the trademark for
Penguin books. He lectured at Chelsea School
of Art and his work has been exhibited
worldwide.*

1 *POSTER:*
LONDON PASSENGER TRANSPORT
BOARD

DATE: 1936

2 *POSTER:*
LONDON TRANSPORT

DATE: 1936

3 *POSTER:*
LONDON UNDERGROUND

DATE: 1935

4 *POSTER:* SHELL FUEL

DATE: 1938

5 *POSTER:* LONDON TRANSPORT

DATE: 1939

6 *PUBLIC INFORMATION POSTER*

DATE: c. 1938

3

4

5

6

BURKHARD MANGOLD
(1873–1950)

*Born in Basle, Switzerland. Studied at the
German School of Art in Basle and the
Conservatory of Art in Zurich, under Dr
Oskar Bätschmann. He taught for three years
before travelling to Paris in 1894, where he
began painting, and subsequently to Munich,
where he mastered the technical skills of
lithography. In 1900 he returned to Basle and
began producing posters with a graphic artist
called Anstalten Wassermann. Mangold was
extremely versatile and employed a broad
range of styles to suit differing subjects. In
1905 an exhibition of his work was held in
Zurich and over the following 15 years he
established himself as one of the most
important poster artists of his generation,
producing some of his finest work in the years
before World War I. In 1915 he returned to the
German School of Art in Basle to study
stained glass design and lithography and was
president of the school from 1918-29.*

I *ADVERTISEMENT*
DATE:1902

2 *ADVERTISEMENT*
DATE:1916

1

    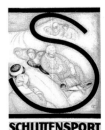

2

1

2

3

BETTY SWANWICK (b. 1915)

Born in London. Studied at Goldsmith's College School of Art, The Royal College of Art and the Central School of Arts and Crafts in London. Her books as author and illustrator include The Cross-Purposes *(1945),* Ella's Birthday *(1946) and* Beauty and the Burglar *(1958). She contributed to* Country Fair *and* The Strand Magazine. *Her quirky,* faux-naif *style was used to good effect in London Transport posters during the late 1930s, including "London Transport for all occasions", depicting a wedding in which the bride and groom are upstaged by several pale bridesmaids and five angular black cats. Animals were favourite subjects and another London Transport poster, "To the fields", shows a complex pattern of horses and frolicking rabbits, typically combining an aura of innocence with a sharp visual wit.*

1 *POSTER:* LONDON TRANSPORT
DATE: NOT KNOWN

2 *POSTER:* LONDON TRANSPORT
DATE: 1938

3 *POSTER:* LONDON TRANSPORT
DATE: 1938

WILLIAM HEATH ROBINSON
(1872–1944)

*Born in London. After studying at the Royal
Academy Schools he began illustrating books,
including two children's books of his own,* Uncle
Lubin *(1902) and* Bill the Minder *(1912).
During World War I he emerged as one of the
greatest comic artists of his time with his
whimsical pen and ink drawings of incredibly
complicated contraptions usually designed to solve
very simple problems. These drawings can be seen
in* The Saintly Hum *(1917),* Humours of Golf
(1923), Absurdities *(1934) and the* Professor
Branestawm *books (1933), which finally
made him the most famous of the three
Robinson brothers, the others being Tom and
Charles. Between the wars he contributed to
such periodicals as* The Bystander, The
Sketch, The Humorist, The Graphic *and*
The Strand, *and exhibited a mural for the
liner* Empress of Britain. *He worked
mainly in black and white, and had a highly
developed eye for detail and characterization.*

❚ *BOOK:*
THE INCREDIBLE ADVENTURES
OF PROFESSOR BRANESTAWM

DATE: 1933

1

2

THE KUKRYNIKSY

A group of Russian artists comprising Mikhail Kupriyanov (b. 1903), Porfiry Krylov (b. 1902) and Nikolai Sokolov (b. 1903). They studied at Vkhutemas in Moscow, where they were pupils of David Moor. During the 1920s they began to collaborate on student publications, first of all as "the Kukryniks", and, after 1927, as "the Kukryniksy". From 1933 their cartoons began to appear regularly in Pravda *and their satirical drawings were much in demand by leading newspapers and magazines. Their poster, "We shall mercilessly defeat and destroy the enemy", was one of the first to appear within a few days of Hitler's invasion and throughout World War II they made a significant contribution to Soviet political poster design. They were also prominent book illustrators.*

1 *CARICATURE:*
(published in Moscow)

DATE: c. 1940

2 *CARICATURE:*
(published in Moscow)

DATE: c. 1940

3 *CARICATURE:*
(published in Moscow)

DATE: c. 1940

3

1

JOHN HEARTFIELD
(1891–1968)

Born Helmut Herzfelde in Berlin. Studied at the School of Applied Arts in Munich and the Arts and Crafts School in Berlin. Later he Anglicized his name as a protest against German militarism. In 1911 he was one of the founders of the Berlin Dada group, and is renowned as the greatest exponent of photomontage — the technique of combining strikingly incongruous photographic images to surreal effect. An active member of the Communist Party from 1918, he co-edited the satirical journals Jedermann Sein Eigener Fussball *and* Die Pleite *with Grosz and his brother, Wieland Herzfelde, and from 1923-27 was editor of the satirical magazine* Der Knüppel. *His anti-Nazi images, which appeared in most of the newspapers and magazines of the political left in Germany from the 1920s, lost him his German nationality in 1934. He was eventually forced to move to Czechoslovakia and then to Britain, where he worked for* Picture Post *and* Lilliput *magazines and Penguin Books. He returned to East Berlin in 1950. In 1956 he was nominated by Bertolt Brecht to the German Academy of Arts, where he became a professor.*

1 *ORIGINAL PHOTOMONTAGE:*
"BLOOD AND IRON"

DATE: c. 1935

2 *ORIGINAL PHOTOMONTAGE*

DATE: 1933

3 *ORIGINAL PHOTOMONTAGE*

DATE: 1934

4 *ORIGINAL PHOTOMONTAGE*

DATE: c. 1935

5 *MAGAZINE:* ARENA

DATE: 1927

Deutfche
Eicheln
1933

2

3

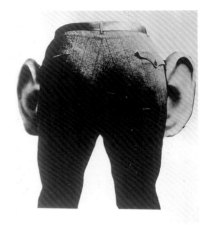

4

5

EDWARD McKNIGHT KAUFFER
(1890–1954)

Born in Montana, USA. He attended evening classes at the Mark Hopkins Institute, where he met Professor Joseph McKnight, who sponsored him to study art in Paris and whose name Kauffer adopted in tribute. From 1926-31 he was involved in theatre and exhibition design, interior design and book illustration. A great fan of T S Eliot's, he illustrated several of his books, including A Song for Simeon *(1925),* Ariel Poems *(1927) and* Marina *(1930). Such was Eliot's satisfaction that he wrote to Kauffer: "Yours is the only kind of decoration I can endure." According to the art historian Anthony Blunt, Kauffer's posters and illustrations took the conventions of super-realism and cubism and broadened their appeal to an otherwise disinterested public. He spent two years in Paris before settling in London in 1914, where his posters for the Underground Railways and Shell Petroleum made him a national figure by the 1920s.*

1 *BOOK:*
ELSIE AND THE CHILD
by Arnold Bennett

DATE: 1924

2 *POSTER:*
LONDON TRANSPORT

DATE: 1932

3 *TRAVEL POSTER*

DATE: c. 1924

4 *POSTER:*
LONDON TRANSPORT

DATE: 1934

5 *POSTER:*
LONDON TRANSPORT

DATE: 1932

6 *ADVERTISEMENT:*
SHELL FUEL

DATE: 1939

1

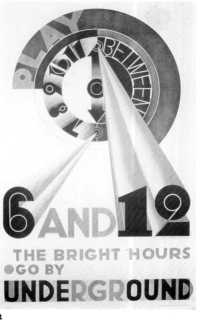

2

3

4

5

6

MAURITS CORNELIS ESCHER
(1898–1972)

Born in Leeuwarden, Holland. Studied graphics at the Technical School of Architecture and Ornamental Design in Haarlem. Between 1922 and 1935 he experimented with various graphic techniques, producing about 70 woodcuts and 40 lithographs during this period. From 1938 he developed highly decorative designs that involved transformations of form through mathematically precise progressions. He also produced a series of geometric drawings, with such titles as "The Regular Division Of A Plane" *and* "Cubic Space-division", *which were of particular interest to mathematicians: a large number of them were exhibited at the International Mathematical Congress in Amsterdam in 1964. His hyper-realistic style had the surreal effect of confusing the real with the imaginary, as in his complex and highly detailed visual illusions which use tricks of line and perspective to create images of the impossible. Since his death, his work has frequently been used to illustrate album covers, books and magazine articles and his visual ideas have been a source of inspiration to photographers as well as illustrators.*

1 *WOODCUT:* "DAY AND NIGHT"

DATE: 1938

2 *WOODCUT:* "DEVELOPMENT 1"

DATE: 1937

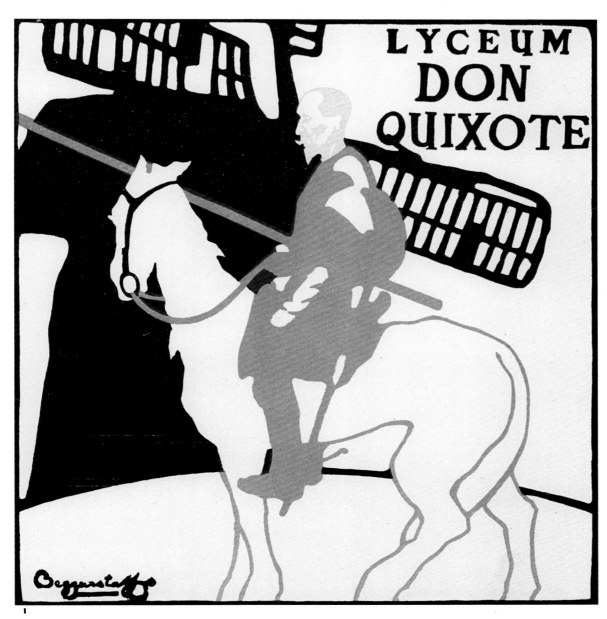

THE BEGGARSTAFFS

Sir William Nicholson (1872–1949) and James Pryde (1886–1941). Although referred to as "The Beggarstaff Brothers", William Nicholson and James Pryde were in fact brothers-in-law. Nicholson was born in Newark-on-Trent, UK, and studied at the Académie Julien in Paris. Pryde, born in St Andrews, Scotland, studied at the Royal Scottish Academy School, in Paris under Bouguereau and then also at the Académie Julien. Their collaboration started when they entered a poster competition at the Westminister Aquarium. For economy's sake they worked in one colour and painted in silhouette for ease of reproduction. The ensuing success in the competition and the style that emerged from its constraints made them the most popular artists in Britain. As well as designing posters they both worked in theatre design and Nicholson was also a landscape, still-life and portrait painter who illustrated An Alphabet *(1898) and Siegfried Sassoon's* Memoirs of a Fox-Hunting Man *(1929).*

1 *THEATRE POSTER*

DATE: c. 1900

2 *PUBLICITY POSTER:* HARPER'S MAGAZINE

DATE: c. 1900

3 *POSTCARD:* "CELEBRATED POSTERS" SERIES

DATE: c. 1900

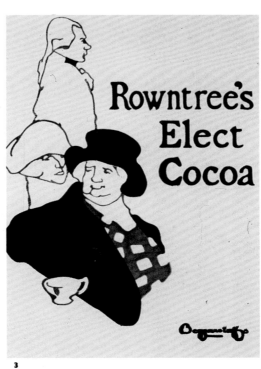

1

DAVID MOOR (1883–1946)

*Born Dmitri Stakhievich Orlov in Russia.
Studied law at Moscow university and
dreamed of being an opera singer. However,
after joining an insurgent group during the
Moscow uprising of 1905, he helped to set up
an underground print shop. The following
year, an idle sketch he had made of a Tsarist
minister was discovered by the editor of an
evening newspaper and led to his first
commission. He became a political cartoonist
and produced a satirical review called*
Volynka *that never passed the censors. After
the October Revolution Moor concentrated on
poster art and throughout the civil war years
produced over 50 political posters. He always
signed them, originally with the name Dor
(an abbreviation of his real name), then Mor
(to avoid confusion with a prominent
journalist) and finally Moor (after a character
in Schiller's play* The Robbers*). He was
strongly influenced by French painting,
German graphic art and by the cartoonist Olaf
Gulbransson.*

I *POSTER:*
"TSARIST REGIMENTS &
THE RED ARMY:
WHAT THEY FOUGHT FOR
BEFORE/WHAT THEY FIGHT FOR
NOW"

DATE: 1919

2 *POSTER:*
"RED SOLDIER UNCLOAKS
WRANGEL TO REVEAL
CONSPIRACY OF WESTERN
NATIONS AGAINST RUSSIA"

DATE: 1920

2

1

2

3

4

VIKTOR NIKOLAEVICH DENI
(1893–1946)

Born Viktor Denisov in Moscow. At the age of 17 he had his first drawings published in the satirical journal Budilink, *for which his older brother wrote poetry. In 1913 he moved to St Petersburg, where his work appeared regularly in the satirical journals* Solntse Rossii, Vesna *and* Satirikon, *and became art director of the humorous weekly* Bich. *When the magazine was closed down after the October Revolution, Deni began working for the artistic section of the Volga military district, making nearly 50 political posters between 1918 and 1921 and becoming one of the leading figures in Soviet poster art (the other was David Moor), particularly admired for his satirical eye. From 1921 he concentrated on drawing newspaper cartoons, contributing regularly to* Pravda, *the Party newspaper, until World War II, when he went back to making posters.*

1 *POSTER:* "DEMKEN'S BAND"

DATE: 1919

2 *POSTER:*
"AT THE GRAVE OF COUNTER-REVOLUTION"

DATE: 1920

3 *POSTER:* "CAPITAL"

DATE: 1919

4 *POSTER:*
"CONSTITUENT ASSEMBLY MEETING"

DATE: 1921

AS FAR AS ILLUSTRATION WAS CONCERNED, the onset of World War II presented a set of opportunities as well as a set of limitations. The need for propaganda, morale boosting and public information material generated a great deal of work. Surprisingly, advertising also thrived during this period. Many manufacturers were concerned that the public would forget them while their production was limited and so ran long-term branding campaigns that stressed their own efforts in the war and assured customers that both quality and supply would be restored as soon as the war had ended.

But while the conflict kept artists busy, the shortages of working materials had a direct effect on their style and methods of working. Paper shortages necessitated that magazines be printed on thinner stock, and art directors advised their illustrators to avoid heavy contrast in their images as the darker areas would print through and appear on the other side of the page. It also became common to print on the reverse side of unused posters, and this encouraged artists to use darker colours to ensure that the old image could not be seen.

With the end of the war, the mid-1940s became boom years for the illustrator in America. During this period of social reconstruction, publishers placed a great emphasis on "lifestyle", and developed a close relationship with the American housewife through magazines such as *Cosmopolitan* and *Ladies' Home Journal,* which featured the work of artists such as John La Gatta and Jon Whitcomb. At the same time, Norman Rockwell was becoming famous for his portraits of American life, which were featured regularly on the covers of the *Saturday Evening Post.* Advertising budgets rocketed, and the hyper-realistic effect of the airbrush challenged photography in the multitude of campaigns mounted by the fast-growing motor car industry. Even the illustrated novel enjoyed a revival with the arrival of the book club.

The 1950s, however, saw a reaction against slick, photograph-oriented realism. The invention of television had a disastrous effect on the publishing business, and several national periodicals folded. There was also a sharp decline in the sale of illustrated books, due to the prevalent belief that a novelist's imagination should be interpreted by the reader and not by an illustrator. In aesthetic terms these problems created a very positive energy and response as publishers adopted a more progressive attitude and took artistic risks in the hope of regaining their fickle public. The result was a diversity of styles, which was encouraged also by the presence of European artists, such as George Grosz, who had emigrated to America at the end of World War II.

Throughout this time in Britain, the illustrator's life had been running on a parallel course to that on the other side of the Atlantic. During the war years, government spending had encouraged the work of many artists, including Abram Games, Tom Eckersley, McKnight Kauffer and Fougasse and, with the return of peace, advertising clients clamoured for their services. In their hands, and with the sponsorship of major companies such as Shell, the poster regained its status as an art form.

There was also something of a revival of book illustration within the Neo-Romantic style. This lasted for about 12 years and began with the publication in 1943 of Mervyn Peake's illustrations for Coleridge's *Rime of the Ancient Mariner*. However, the introduction of British television in the 1950s damaged the publishing industry in much the way it had done in America, although it led to an increased circulation of the *Radio Times* magazine, which was then, and remains, a particularly good medium for the introduction of new illustrator's work.

The complacency, born of prosperity, that suffused this period could never have prepared either artists or the public for the style revolution that was to take place in the 1960s.

Pop Art actually began its life in 1956, not in America but in Britain, with Richard Hamilton's photomontages parodying the domestic and materialistic lifestyle of the time. His work, and that of others in the Independent Group, was further developed in the early '60s by artists such as David Hockney, Patrick Caulfield and Allen Jones in the UK and Andy Warhol in America. Simultaneously, Bridget Riley, Peter Sedgley and Piero Dorazio were exploring the optical effects of line and colour first seen in the paintings of the Spanish artist Victor Vasarely. The philosophies and aesthetics of these artists then meshed with the emergence of a counter-culture that expressed its anarchic sensibilities through every conceivable medium: paintings, sculpture, music, illustrations, fashion, underground magazines, poster art, festivals and "happenings".

What followed was an explosion of aesthetic extravagance never seen before. Naturalistic colours were replaced with day-glow psychedelia in the works of Victor Moscoso and Martin Sharp. Michael English's rock n roll posters, which revealed the influence of Art Nouveau, featured convoluted and virtually unreadable hand-rendered lettering. Eclecticism was the guiding principle of the day: Eastern imagery, mysticism and hallucinatory experience were major creative influences in all branches of the arts.

This revolution was not confined to the so-called "underground". It affected every level of society and, through the work of artists such as Milton Glaser and the influential Push Pin Studios, it reached every level of mainstream media. If ever there was a lingering question about the status of the illustrator as artist, it was answered in the 1960s.

CHAPTER THREE

1940-1969

The New York skyline from the decks of *Queen Elizabeth* as she leaves Pier 90—a sketch by Francis Marshall

FRANCIS MARSHALL (1901–1980)

Studied at the Slade School of Fine Art. Marshall developed a very fluid black-and-white style in charcoal and pen and ink, which earned him many commissions for fashion illustrations in the 1950s. His drawings were full of movement and captured the energy and elegance of the catwalk models and of the era, and his work dominated the pages of Vogue, Harper's Bazaar *and* Woman's Journal. *In 1950 he wrote and illustrated* Sketching the Ballet, *and later produced similar volumes entitled* Fashion Drawing *and* Drawing the Female Figure. *In his manual* Magazine Illustration *(1959) he encouraged the use of photographs as reference material and recommended the special "incident" studios that were then producing images for illustrators. He was also an accomplished watercolourist and landscape artist and exhibited several times at London's Walker Galleries.*

1 *MAGAZINE:*
WOMAN'S MAGAZINE

DATE: c. 1950

2 *MAGAZINE:*
WOMAN'S MAGAZINE

DATE: 1950

FEBRUARY 1950
ONE SHILLING

JOHN LA GATTA (1894–1977)

Born in Naples, Italy. Emigrated to America and studied at the Chase School, New York School of Applied and Fine Arts, Parsons and the Art Students League. He began his career in advertising illustration before establishing his own studio in Woodstock, where he specialized in illustrations of beautiful women. Advised by his wife and model, Florence, his drawings of romantic interludes among the upper classes regularly illustrated the stories in magazines such as Redbook, Ladies' Home Journal *and* Cosmopolitan *and he received many commissions in the early years of World War II. In 1941 he moved to California, where he took up portraiture and landscape painting.*

1 *MAGAZINE:* REDBOOK
DATE: c. 1940

2 *MAGAZINE:* COSMOPOLITAN
DATE: 1949

3 *MAGAZINE:* REDBOOK
DATE: c. 1940

1

2

3

4

5

6

7

ANDRE FRANCOIS (b. c. 1915)

Born in Timisoara, Hungary. Studied in Budapest, then under Cassandre in Paris. From 1944 he established himself as a humorous artist, and his distinctive, satirical images have appeared in magazines such as Punch, Vogue *and* New Yorker. *His advertising posters for Citroën and Kodak are among the most innovative and influential of the 20th century. François has also been a sculptor and poster artist, and designed stage sets and costumes for the theatre and ballet.*

His own illustrated books include The Tattooed Sailor and Other Cartoons from France *(1953),* The Half-naked Knight *(1958),* The Biting Eye *(1960) and* Les Rhumes *(1966). He also illustrated* Ubu Roi *by Alfred Jarry (1957).*

1 *ADVERTISEMENT:* CITROËN CARS

DATE: 1960

2 *ADVERTISEMENT:* CITROËN CARS

DATE: 1960

3 *MAGAZINE:* THE NEW YORKER

DATE: 1965

4 "FIRST AID FOR THE DROWNED" *(unpublished)*

DATE: 1947

5 *MAGAZINE:* PUNCH

DATE: 1955

6 *MAGAZINE:* PUNCH

DATE: 1960

7 "BIG RED BICYCLE" *(unpublished)*

DATE: 1955

TOM ECKERSLEY (b. 1914)

Born in Lancashire, UK. Trained at Salford School of Art under Martin Tyas. He moved to London in 1934 and set up in partnership with Eric Lombers. In 1935 he won the Heywood Medal of Merit for poster design and from 1937-39 he taught poster art at Westminster School of Art. Like his contemporary, Abram Games, Eckersley produced posters with simple graphic imagery, integrated typography, clean lines and strong colours. During World War II he produced cartographical drawings for the Royal Air Force, returning to freelance design in 1945. His style attracted many advertising clients, including Gillette, Guinness, British Aluminium, Eno's and various cigarette brands. In 1948 he was awarded the OBE for his services to British poster design and in 1958 became Head of Graphic Design at the London College of Printing.

I *PUBLIC INFORMATION POSTER:*
ROYAL SOCIETY FOR THE PREVENTION OF ROAD ACCIDENTS, LONDON

DATE: 1944

2 *WWII POSTER:*
POST OFFICE SAVINGS BANK

DATE: 1943

YOU ARE BEING FOLLOWED

USE YOUR DRIVING MIRROR

I

HIS ACTION STATION

SAVING IS EVERYBODY'S WAR JOB POST OFFICE SAVINGS BANK

2

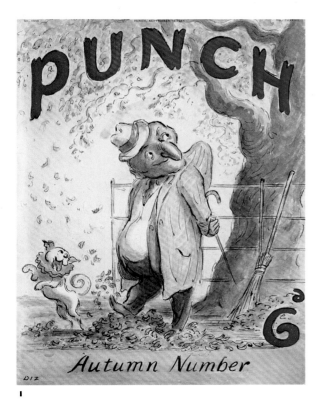

SHOVE HA'PENNY

Dick Nyren was a cricketer
Of very wide renown,
And he shoved a pretty ha'penny
Below Broad Ha'penny Down.

Tom Cribb he was a fighter,
His nose got bashed about,
And he shoved a pretty ha'penny
When he didn't knock it out.

And if these great men wearied,
And their aim grew less than true,
They could always call for Guinness
(There is nothing like a Guinness),
They must have known that Guinness
Is extremely good for you.

EDWARD ARDIZZONE (1900–1979)

Born in Haiphong, Vietnam. His family moved to England when he was five. Attended life classes at Westminster School of Art, under Bernard Meninsky, while employed as a clerk in the City. At the age of 27 he gave up his job to become an artist, and around 1930 began illustrating regularly for the Radio Times. *His books* Little Tim and the Brave Sea Captain *(1936) and* Lucy Brown and Mr Grimes *(1937), which he wrote and illustrated to entertain his own children, were a great success in England and America and* Tim All Alone *(1956), was the first book to win the British Library Association's Kate Greenaway Medal. He is best known as a children's illustrator, but his fluid and expressive style, either drawn with cross-hatching or painted in simple watercolours, was equally suited to serious subjects. He cited Bernard Meninsky, Doré, Daumier and Caldecott as his main influences. He was an Official War Artist during World War II and the drawings he made then remain a powerful record of the atrocities of war.*

1 *ADVERTISEMENT:*
PUNCH MAGAZINE

DATE: 1954

2 *ADVERTISEMENT:*
GUINNESS BEER

DATE: 1955

3 *ADVERTISEMENT:*
GUINNESS BEER

DATE: 1955

4 *BOOK:*
TIM ALL ALONE
by Edward Ardizzone

DATE: 1956

MERVYN PEAKE (1911–1968)

Born in Kuling, China, the son of medical missionaries. The family returned to England in 1923 and he was educated at Eltham College, Kent, and the Royal Academy Schools in London. His first illustrated book, Captain Slaughterboard, *a humorous fantasy for children, was published in 1939. Invalided out of the forces in 1943, he visited Germany in 1946 to record the devastation for* Leader *magazine. He was also sent to make drawings at Belsen — an experience which profoundly affected his later work. Peake illustrated many books, including* Alice Through the Looking Glass *(1954),* Grimm's Fairy Tales *and* Treasure Island. *He also wrote and illustrated his own novels and poems, including* Rhymes Without Reason *(1944),* Captain Slaughterboard Drops Anchor *(1945),* Shapes and Sounds *(1941) and* The Glassblowers *(1950). His most famous work,* Gormenghast *(part two of a gothic fantasy trilogy written between 1946 and 1959) won the W J Heinemann Foundation Prize (Royal Society of Literature) in 1950. In many of Peake's works a lively humour is merged with an instinct for the macabre and the grotesque, as seen in the facial caricatures that were a recurring element in his work.*

1, 4—6 *BOOK:* RIDE-A-COCK HORSE & OTHER NURSERY RHYMES
DATE: 1945
2, 7 *BOOK:* FIGURES OF SPEECH *by Mervyn Peake*
DATE: 1952
3 *BOOK:* TITUS ALONE *by Mervyn Peake*
DATE: 1959

1

Coming up to scratch

2

3

4

5

6

Burning their bridges

7

PHILIP GOUGH (b. 1908)

Born in Warrington, Cheshire, UK. Studied at art schools in Liverpool, London and Penzance and trained as a stage designer in Liverpool. In 1928 he designed the sets for A Midsummer Night's Dream *at Liverpool Repertory Theatre and in 1929 designed the sets for the original production of* Toad of Toad Hall. *Moving to London, he worked in a commercial studio for two years and then began designing for the London theatres, working on over 25 productions until after World War II, when he turned to book and magazine illustration.*

1 *BOOK:*
THE NEW BOOK OF DAYS
DATE: 1941

2, 3 *BOOK:*
HANS ANDERSEN'S FAIRY TALES
DATE: 1946

1

2

3

ROWLAND HILDER (b. 1905)

Born in Long Island, USA, but settled in England during childhood. Studied at Goldsmith's College School of Art, London, and won a travelling scholarship which he applied to studying marine art in the Netherlands. From 1925 he received commissions from publishers, many with marine themes, including Moby Dick *(1926) and* The Adventures of a Trafalgar Lad *(1926). His landscape drawings for Mary Webb's* Precious Bane *(1929) were later marketed as greetings cards. Other significant titles were* The Midnight Folk *(1931), a personal commission from poet laureate John Masefield,* The Bible for Today *(1938) and, with his wife Edith Hilder, the* Shell Guide to Flowers of the Countryside. *His prolific output of greetings card designs for the Medici Society and Ward Gallery established his widespread popularity, but after World War II he published his designs through his own Heron Press. From the 1960s he became increasingly more dedicated to painting for non-commercial reasons, though his work continued to be widely reproduced.*

I *MAGAZINE:* PUNCH

DATE: 1952

2, 3 *BOOK:* TREASURE ISLAND
by Robert Louis Stevenson

DATE: 1946

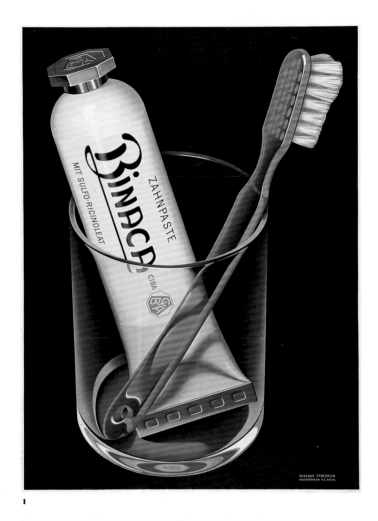

NIKLAUS STOECKLIN
(1896–1982)

Born in Basel, Switzerland. Studied at art schools in Munich and Basel. He was a major figure in the development of Swiss poster art, which had already achieved high standards by the 1920s. His work produced a refinement of design concepts, ranging from stylized, two-dimensional, almost purely symbolic images to more detailed and realistic representations, married to clean, unfussy typographic presentation. Examples can be seen in museums in Basel and Zurich, and Stoecklin's work has gone into private collections worldwide. Another important interest was postage stamp design and he produced a number of detailed designs for this purpose, mainly featuring plants and animals. He also illustrated books, including Hermann Hesse's Knulp *(1945).*

1 *ADVERTISEMENT:*
BINACA TOOTHPASTE

DATE: 1941

2 *ADVERTISEMENT:*
META MATCH STRIKERS

DATE: 1941

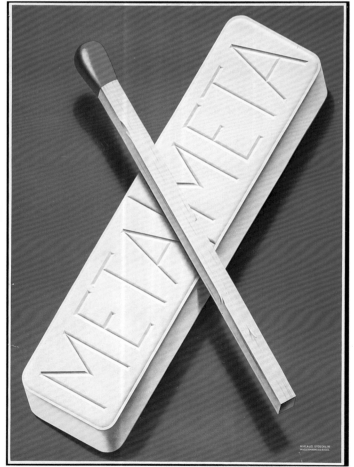

HOLYHEAD

LMS R.M.S. "HIBERNIA" IRISH MAIL SERVICE

By NORMAN WILKINSON, R.I.

Holyhead in Anglesey is the port of departure of the LMS Steamers for Ireland. A passenger service, carrying the Royal Mails, leaves twice daily for Kingstown and there is a regular cargo service for Dublin. Holyhead is conveniently situated for those wishing to take a holiday in Anglesey, and has a comfortable Hotel owned by the LMS.

1

A FEW
**CARELESS WORDS
MAY END IN THIS—**

Many lives were lost in the last war through careless talk
Be on your guard ! Don't discuss movements of ships or troops

2

LMS MENAI STRAITS FROM THE TUBULAR BRIDGE
EUSTON — HOLYHEAD LINE
By NORMAN WILKINSON, R.I.

3

NORMAN WILKINSON (1878–1971)

Born in Cambridge, UK. Studied painting at art schools in England and Paris. After settling in London, from 1901 he worked on The Illustrated London News, *an association lasting almost 15 years. He also contributed to* The Graphic, The Harmsworth Magazine *and* The Illustrated Mail. *He was an accomplished marine painter and his book illustrations covered naval subjects, landscapes and angling themes.* Landscapes and Seascapes *(1929) and* Ships in Pictures *(1944) were among his own published titles. During both World Wars he designed the camouflage used by British Navy ships. It was at Wilkinson's suggestion that in the 1920s London Midland & Scottish Railways commissioned posters from a number of notable artists of the day, including Fred Taylor and Tom Purvis. His own "Galloway" (1924) is a graphic portrait of the rich colour and expanse of the Scottish highlands. He was also commissioned for poster work by the shipping company Cunard.*

1 *TRAVEL POSTER:*
LONDON MIDLAND & SCOTTISH
RAILWAY COMPANY

DATE: 1940

2 *PUBLIC INFORMATION POSTER*

DATE: 1940

3 *TRAVEL POSTER:*
LONDON MIDLAND & SCOTTISH
RAILWAY COMPANY

DATE: NOT KNOWN

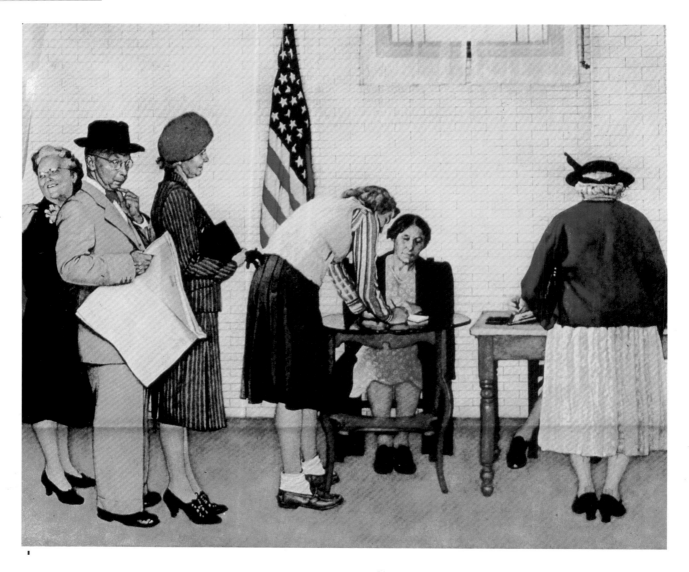

1

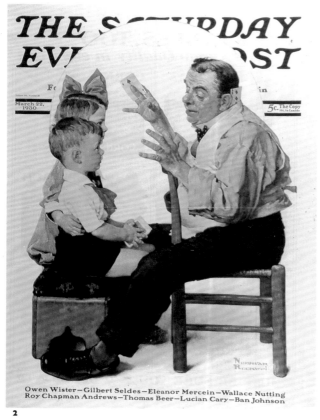

2

3

4

5

NORMAN ROCKWELL (1894–1979)

Born in New York. Studied at Chase Art School, the National Academy of Design and the Art Students League in New York, under Thomas Fogarty and George Bridgman. At the age of 17 he was already illustrating for McBride and Nast publications and later became editor of a boy scout's magazine. His covers for The Saturday Evening Post, *spanning more than 40 years from 1916, made him one of America's best-known and most loved illustrators. His superbly crafted portrayals of American life were done with a warmth and humour that touched the hearts of millions and reflected the spirit of the country at the time. During World War II the essence of Franklin D Roosevelt's war aims was captured in Rockwell's powerful* Four Freedoms *posters, one of which is on permanent display at the Metropolitan Museum of Art, New York.*

1 *MAGAZINE:*
THE SATURDAY EVENING POST

DATE: 1940

2 *MAGAZINE:*
THE SATURDAY EVENING POST

DATE: c. 1940

3 *POSTER:*

DATE: c.1945

4 *MAGAZINE:*
THE SATURDAY EVENING POST

DATE: 1940

5 *MAGAZINE:*
THE SATURDAY EVENING POST

DATE: 1949

1

BEN SHAHN (b. 1898) ·

Born in Kovno, Russia. His family emigrated to America in 1904 and he studied biology at New York University and attended the National Academy of Design. In the 1920s he travelled in Europe and North Africa and during World War II he designed posters for various government departments. His work, which uses heavy outlines to expressive effect and which brings to mind the illustrations of François and Buffet, has won numerous awards. He has illustrated several children's books, including A Partridge in a Pear Tree *(1949), which featured illustrations in a style that was most unusual for the world of the nursery rhyme. His adult publications include* The Sorrows of Priapus *(1957) by E Dahlberg and* Thirteen Poems *(1956) by Wilfred Owen. His work has also appeared in advertising campaigns and in publications such as* Fortune Magazine, Harper's Bazaar *and* Town and Country. *He is a painter as well as an illustrator and has had one-man shows in Boston, New York and Chicago.*

1 *WWII POSTER*

DATE: 1943

2 *WWII POSTER*

DATE: 1943

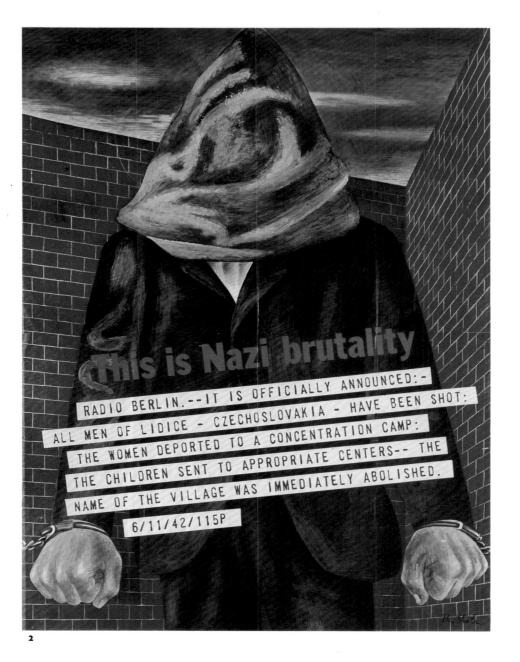

2

1

2

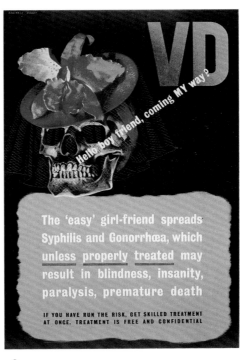

3

REGINALD MOUNT (1906—1979)

Born in London. Studied at Leyton School of Art. Mount worked at Greenly's studio in London, then as a visualiser at the Lintas advertising agency, before being employed at Odhams Press Ltd as a general artist and designer. During World War II he worked for the Ministry of Information, where he produced some of Britain's finest war posters, including the salvage, security and diptheria immunisation campaigns and the first national anti-VD campaign in 1943-44. He also designed the "Liberation of France" poster for the D-Day landings. After the war he worked as a freelance designer in house-styling, packaging, publicity and exhibitions, while continuing part-time at what became the Central Office of Information. With Eileen Evans, he produced an enormous body of work, including award-winning posters for the anti-smoking and road safety campaigns and the now classic "Keep Britain Tidy" campaign. In 1957 he was awarded the OBE for services to government publicity.

1 *FILM POSTER:* LADYKILLERS

DATE: 1955

2 *GOVERNMENT INFORMATION POSTER*

DATE: 1962

3 *GOVERNMENT INFORMATION POSTER*

DATE: 1943

FOUGASSE (1887–1965)

Born Cyril Kenneth Bird, in London, and educated at Cheltenham College and King's College, London. From 1916 his work was published in Punch *and in 1937 he became its Art Editor, then Editor (1949–52). He illustrated a number of books, including* The Luck of the Draw *(1936),* Drawing the Line Somewhere *(1937) and* The Good Tempered Pencil *(1956). During World War II he designed posters for various government ministries, including the famous "Careless Talk Costs Lives" series for the Ministry of Information. Fougasse was a master of the expressive line. Over the years he developed a highly individual graphic shorthand in his drawings of humorous figures, the hands and feet often represented by a single line.*

1 *WWII POSTER*

DATE: 1940

2 *WWII POSTER*

DATE: 1940

3 *POSTER:*
LONDON UNDERGROUND

DATE: c. 1940

4 *POSTER:*
NATIONAL SOCIETY FOR THE
PREVENTION OF CRUELTY TO
CHILDREN

DATE: c. 1940

1

2

3

4

"HAND UP THE GIRL WHO BURNT DOWN THE EAST WING LAST NIGHT"

Ronald Searle

RONALD SEARLE (b. 1920)

Born in Cambridge, UK. Studied at Cambridge School of Art and first started drawing for the Cambridge Daily News *in 1935. In 1939 he fought in Malaya and was imprisoned by the Japanese from 1942 onwards, an experience which he cites as a major formative experience. His first published book after the war,* Forty Drawings of Ronald Searle *(1946), was a sobering record of this bleak interlude in his life. However, he is more famous for having created the St Trinian's schoolgirls in his books* Hurrah for St Trinian's *(1948),* The Female Approach *(1948),* Back to the Slaughterhouse, *(1952) and* The Terror of St Trinian's *(1952). In 1956 he joined the staff of* Punch *magazine, a perfect platform for his witty observations on social behaviour. His work also had a serious side and he was a member of the Association of International Artists, a political group. In 1969 he produced* The Secret Sketchbook: The Backstreets of Hamburg, *which contained no text but a series of expressive sketches of prostitutes which owe something to the influence of George Grosz. His work has appeared in many of the major British publications and was frequently published in America's* Saturday Evening Post.

1 *ADVERTISEMENT*

DATE: 1960

2 "THE COMING OF THE GREAT CAT GOD"

DATE: 1968

3 "ST TRINIAN'S"

DATE: c. 1948-1952

NOEL FONTANET (1898–1982)

Born in Germany. Studied at the Geneva Art School and later drew for local newspapers and produced caricatures for the Nebelspalter. He was an excellent draughtsman and developed a strong graphic style which earned him the position of art director in a design company, and fame as a poster artist.

1 *POSTER:* "GENEVA INTERNATIONAL AUTOMOBILE SHOW"

DATE: 1930

2 *ADVERTISEMENT:* VELOSOLEX

DATE: 1950

3 *POSTER:* "GIVE BOOKS"

DATE: 1943

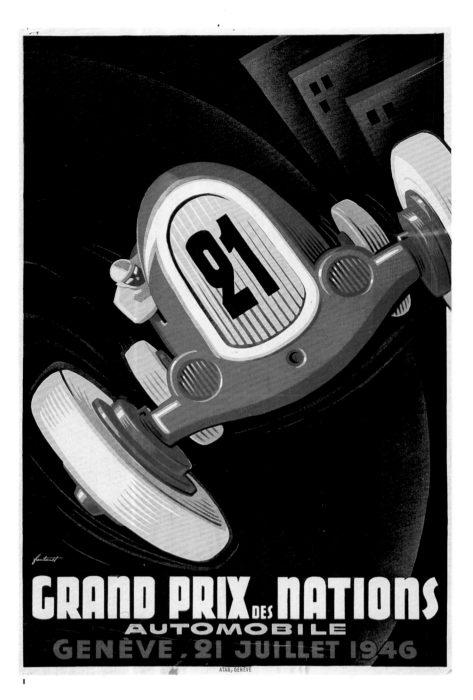

1

2

3

1

2

KEITH VAUGHAN (1912–1977)

Born in Sussex, UK. He received no formal art training, but during the 1930s he developed an interest in modern art, particularly the work of Cézanne, Picasso and the French Impressionists. During World War II he worked as a clerk and German interpreter in London and produced a huge volume of powerful gouaches and ink drawings which were displayed as part of a war exhibition at the National Gallery. His first one-man show was in 1944 and it was at this time that he met Graham Sutherland and John Minton. During the 1950s his work, although essentially figurative, became more abstract and revealed the influence of De Stael and the Abstract Expressionists. He had several major exhibitions and taught periodically at the Camberwell, Central and Slade Schools of Art. In 1964 he was made an Honorary Fellow of the Royal College of Art and in 1965 was awarded the CBE. His Journals and Drawings *was published the following year and in 1989 there was a major retrospective of his work at the Austin/Desmond Gallery in London.*

1 "LANDSCAPE"
(unpublished)

DATE: 1949

2 "THE WOODMAN"
(unpublished)

DATE: 1949

CHARLES KEEPING (b. 1924)

Born in London. The son of a professional boxer, he grew up around the street markets of south London. After World War II he studied drawing, etching, engraving and lithography at the Regent Street Polytechnic, where he returned in 1956 as a lecturer. Keeping works mostly in pen and ink and has illustrated over 150 books, including Charlie, Charlotte and the Golden Canary, *which won the Kate Greenaway Medal in 1967, and* The Wildman, *which won the Francis Williams Prize in 1976.* Joseph's Yard *(1969),* The God Beneath the Sea *(1970) and* The Railway Passage *(1974) were all commended for the Kate Greenaway Medal. He has taught at Camberwell School of Art since 1979 and his work is represented at the Victoria & Albert Museum in London.*

1 "COSTER CART"
(unpublished)

DATE: 1956

2 "DERELICT CITY CARTS"
(unpublished)

DATE: 1954

1

2

NORMAN THELWELL (b.1923)

Born in Birkenhead, UK. He drew from childhood but was not encouraged to consider a career in art and started work in 1939 as a junior office clerk. After World War II a special government grant awarded to ex-servicemen enabled him to study at Liverpool College of Art and after graduating in 1950 he taught at Wolverhampton College of Art. In 1952 he sent his first cartoon to Punch *magazine and in 1956 he left teaching to take up illustration full-time. Over the next 25 years he produced over 60 covers and 1500 illustrations for* Punch, *reflecting the English way of life. He also drew a pony cartoon strip, "Penelope and Kipper", for the* Sunday Express. *Although he is most famous for his humorous cartoons of endearingly scruffy, barrel-chested ponies ridden by tubby little girls, he also drew cartoons on a wide range of serious moral and political issues, but always with his characteristically gentle eye. His books are sold all over the world and his autobiography,* Wrestling with a Pencil, *was published in 1986.*

1 "ACQUIRING A PONY IS NOT AS EASY AS IT SOUNDS"

DATE: 1962

2 "I NEVER TIRE OF LOOKING AT THE SEA"

DATE: 1952

FRANK FRAZETTA (b. 1928)

Born in Brooklyn, New York. At the age of only eight, he enrolled at the Brooklyn Academy of Fine Arts. He started his career working in comics, was an assistant to Al Capp on Li'l Abner *and developed his own strip called* Johnny Comet *as well as contributing to* Mad *and* Playboy. *During the 60s and 70s his cover illustrations for the* Conan *series of heroic fantasy stories by R E Howard brought him to the forefront of science-fiction art. After illustrating the covers for a series of* Tarzan *paperbacks his style changed direction as he became more involved in sword and sorcery illustrations. From this genre Frazetta has emerged as an artist with a cult following. He now has the freedom to choose his own subjects and the originals of his calendars, posters and paperback covers are valuable collectors' pieces. His style, characterized by exotic settings, sex, violence and exaggerated physiques, is definitive of fantasy art and has been enormously influential.* The Fantastic Art of Frank Frazetta *was published in 1975.*

1 *POSTER:*
"FRANKENSTEIN AND DRACULA"
(non-commissioned)

DATE: 1969

2 *POSTER:*
"REASSEMBLED MAN"
(non-commissioned)

DATE: 1965

3 *POSTER:*
"THE RETURN OF JOUGAR"
(non-commissioned)

DATE: 1967

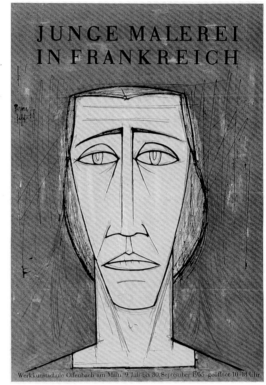

BERNARD BUFFET (b. 1928)

Born in Paris. At 15 he took evening classes in art and spent a year at the Ecole des Beaux-Arts in Paris. In 1947 he held his first exhibition, in a book shop in the Rue des Ecoles, and in 1948 shared the Grand Prix de la Critique. Seven years later his distinctive style won him recognition by the Connaissance des Arts as the leading post-war artist. His illustrated books include Cocteau's La Voix Humaine *(1957),* Cyrano de Bergerac's Les Voyages Fantastiques *(1958) and* Les Chants des Maldoror *(1952). He has also designed stage sets for two ballets:* La Chambre *for Roland Petit and* Le Rendez-vous Manqué, *based on a story by Françoise Sagan. His work is held in permanent collection by the Tate Gallery, London, and the Museum of Modern Art, New York.*

1 *CATALOGUE:* NICOLAS WINE

DATE: 1961

2 *POSTER:*
"YOUNG PAINTER IN FRANCE"

DATE: 1955

3 *PAINTING:* "PIETA"

DATE: 1941

JOAN HASSALL (b. 1906)

Born in London, daughter of the illustrator John Hassall. She studied at the Royal Academy Schools and subsequently attended the London County Council School of Photo-engraving and Lithography. Her first commission after graduating was for a wood-engraved title page for her brother Christopher's book of poems Devil's Dyke *(1936). Other books include* A Child's Garden of Verses *by Robert Louis Stevenson (1947) and Jane Austen's* Mansfield Park *(1959),* Northanger Abbey *(1960),* Persuasion *(1961) and* Emma *(1962). She also illustrated for a number of magazines, including* Argosy, London Mystery Magazine, Picture Post *and* The Periodical, *and designed the invitation for the coronation of Queen Elizabeth II in 1952. Her wood-engraved illustrations are worked in a meticulous style influenced by Thomas Bewick.*

1 *BOOK:* CRANFORD
by Mrs Gaskell

DATE: 1940

2 *BOOK:* SEALSKIN TROUSERS
by Eric Linklater

DATE: 1947

3 *BOOK:* URANIA
by Ruth Pitter

DATE: 1950

4 *BOOK:*
COLLECTED POEMS OF
ANDREW YOUNG

DATE: 1950

1

2

3

4

ABRAM GAMES (b. 1914)

Born in London. Mainly self-taught as an artist, his first job was in a commercial studio from 1932-36, and it was during this period that he developed an interest in poster design. His work, featuring striking colour, bold graphic ideas and beautifully integrated typography, communicated clearly and effectively, and in 1940 he became the official War Office poster designer. At the end of the war he produced posters and stamps for British, Irish, Israeli and Portuguese government departments, and designed murals and advertising poster campaigns for clients such as Guinness, BOAC, Shell and Capstan cigarettes. In 1951 he designed the official emblem for the Festival of Britain and in 1953 the symbol of BBC Television. From 1946-53 he taught at the Royal College of Art in London. He was awarded the OBE in 1958 for his services to graphic design.

1 POSTER:
FINSBURY HEALTH CENTRE

DATE: 1943

2 POSTER:
BRITISH EUROPEAN AIRWAYS

DATE: 1960

3 POSTER:
LONDON TRANSPORT

DATE: 1953

C WALTER HODGES (b. 1909)

Born in Beckenham, UK. Studied at Dulwich College and Goldsmith's College of Art, under Ed Sullivan. After graduation he designed scenery and costumes for the Everyman Theatre in Hampstead, London, then worked briefly in advertising before becoming a freelance illustrator. In 1934 he designed and executed a huge mural at the Museum of the Chartered Insurance Institute of London. From 1936-37 he lived in New York, where he began writing and illustrating children's books. He specialized in historical reconstructions, and the publication of Shakespeare's Theatre *won him the Kate Greenaway Medal for best British book illustration in 1964. In 1966 he was runner-up for the Carnegie Medal for* Namesake. *His love of the stage is quite evident in his work and in 1951 he was involved in the design of the Mermaid Theatre in London.*

1	*MAGAZINE:* RADIO TIMES
	DATE: 1950
2	*MAGAZINE:* RADIO TIMES
	DATE: 1950
3	*MAGAZINE:* RADIO TIMES
	DATE: 1950

Christmas Number with Programmes from Christmas Eve to December 30
WITH FULL DETAILS OF
'Christmas Journey' the world-wide programme preceding the broadcast by
H.M. THE KING

2d

1

2

3

1

VICKY (b. 1913)

Born Victor Weisz in Berlin, of Hungarian parentage. He left school at the age of 14 to help support his family and began selling caricatures of public figures to the local newspapers. With the rise of Nazism he turned to political cartoons in 1929 and in 1935 he left Germany to settle in London, where he became a British citizen. He worked for the News Chronicle *as a staff artist and, in the years after World War II, his drawings illustrated stories and articles in publications such as* Cosmopolitan, Woman's Own, The Leader *and* The Daily Mirror *and in 1958 he joined the staff of the* Evening Standard.

1 *MAGAZINE:* THE LEADER
DATE: 1950

2 *MAGAZINE:* THE LEADER
DATE: 1950

2

1

2

LEONARD BASKIN (b. 1922)

Born in New Brunswick, USA. Studied at Yale University of Fine Arts and the New School for Social Research, and also in Paris and Florence. Sculptor and graphic artist, he has made an important contribution to book illustration as publisher and printer for his own Gehenna Press. The first title of this imprint, On a Pyre of Withered Roses *(1942), was produced while Baskin was still a student at Yale. The range of subsequent work includes strongly graphic linoleum and wood engravings in* A Little Book of Natural History *(1951), and highly detailed etchings in* Horned Beetles and Other Insects *(1958).*

1 "TOBIAS AND THE ANGEL"
(unpublished)

DATE: 1958

2 "MAN WITH SPRING PLANTS"
(unpublished)

DATE: 1953

COBY WHITMORE (b. 1913)

Born in Ohio, USA. Trained at the Dayton Art Institute and the Chicago Art Institute, where he took evening classes while serving an apprenticeship in a local art studio. He worked briefly for the Herald Examiner *before moving to New York. In common with his contemporary, Jon Whitcomb, his primary interest was in depicting glamorous and beautiful women, but his softer use of colour was more definitively romantic and his compositions explored the subtler nuances of the relationships between men and women.*

1 *MAGAZINE:*
LADIES' HOME JOURNAL

DATE: 1947

2 *ILLUSTRATION: (unpublished)*
DATE: NOT KNOWN

3 *MAGAZINE:*
THE SATURDAY EVENING POST

DATE: NOT KNOWN

1

THORNTON UTZ (b. 1914)

Born in Memphis, USA. He was a student of Burton Callicott, whom he cites as his greatest influence, before attending the American Academy of Art in Chicago. He then became a freelance illustrator at the studio partnership of Sundblom, Stevens and Stultz. Although one of the "Sundblom Circle", he developed his own highly individual approach to the problems of illustration. His method is to work out his compositions with quick, rough sketches and then pose and photograph models in the positions that he has drawn. Later, when preparing the final illustration, he uses the photographs to provide details of lighting and minutiae that would otherwise remain unseen. The technique is extremely successful and he has been commissioned frequently by The Saturday Evening Post, Cosmopolitan, Redbook *and* Good Housekeeping. *During the early 50s he travelled to India, Japan, Hong Kong and Hawaii recording the activities of the US Air Force. He now concentrates on commissioned portrait painting.*

1 *MAGAZINE:* SPORTS AFIELD

DATE: 1959

2 *MAGAZINE:*
THE SATURDAY EVENING POST

DATE: 1962

3 *MAGAZINE:*
THE SATURDAY EVENING POST

DATE: 1958

2

3

JON WHITCOMB (b. 1906)

Born in Oklahoma, USA. Studied art at Ohio Wesleyan University, then worked as a poster artist and produced drawings for local advertising agencies. In 1934 he moved to New York and concentrated on freelance illustration. He specialized in depicting romantic interludes and portraits of beautiful, glamorous women and achieved popularity through publication in such magazines as Collier's *and* Good Housekeeping. *He spent some time as a combat artist during World War II, returning to gentler themes after his discharge in 1945. His style was perfectly suited to the editorial content of* Redbook Magazine *and* Cosmopolitan, *for whom he wrote and illustrated a monthly column on movie stars. He has also written two children's books,* Coco *and* Pom Pom's Christmas, *and a book on beautiful women,* All about Girls.

I "BROWN-HAIRED GAL"
(unpublished)

DATE: c. 1940

2 *MAGAZINE:*
WOMAN'S HOME COMPANION

DATE: 1941

EDWARD BAWDEN (b. 1903)

Born in Braintree, UK. Studied at Cambridge School of Art and the Royal College of Art, under Paul Nash. He was an Official War Artist during World War II and travelled to France and the Middle East. His strong graphic style, economy of line and sardonic wit perfectly captured the spirit of the places he visited. Influenced by Nash, Beardsley, Cézanne and Picasso, he has also designed and executed murals for the liner SS Orcades and for the Lion and the Unicorn Pavilion at the Festival of Britain. His illustration clients are many and include Shell, London Transport and Penguin books. He tends to draw in pen and ink with washes on non-absorbent paper. He is also a highly accomplished watercolourist and won the Francis Williams Book Illustration Award in 1977 and 1982. He taught design and book illustration for many years, first at Goldsmith's College and later at the Royal College of Art, and since 1951 has been a trustee of the Tate Gallery, where his work is represented. In 1956 he was made a Royal Academician and is still illustrating today at the age of 86.

1 *POSTER:* LONDON TRANSPORT

DATE: 1952

2 *POSTER:*
LONDON UNDERGROUND

DATE: c. 1950

3 *BOOK:*
LIFE IN AN ENGLISH VILLAGE

DATE: 1949

1

AT THE HORSEGUARDS
WHITEHALL
at 11 a.m. (Sundays at 10 a.m.)
Nearest Stations:—
Westminster and Trafalgar Square.

AT BUCKINGHAM PALACE or
ST JAMES'S PALACE
between 10·30 and 11·15 a.m.
Nearest Stations:—
St James's Park and Dover Street.

CHANGING THE GUARD
LONDON'S DAILY MILITARY TATTOOS

UNDERGROUND

2

3

1

2

3

ALFRED BESTALL (1892–1986)

Born in Burma. Studied at Birmingham School of Art. After World War I he joined a commercial studio and also worked as a freelance illustrator. In 1936 he took over the Rupert Bear strip in the Daily Express *from its original illustrator, Mary Tourtel (1897-1940), and subsequently was identified with Rupert until his retirement in 1965, when he left a great deal of material still to be published. As well as the newspaper strip, Rupert was published in annuals, the first in 1936; at the height of their popularity during the 40s and 50s, they sold over a million and a half copies a year. Bestall followed the graphic style developed by Tourtel, but introduced more humour and action into the storylines, sometimes developing a slightly surreal element to the adventures of the intrepid bear and his playmates.*

1, 2 *BOOK:* DAILY EXPRESS ANNUAL

DATE: 1956

1

2

KATHLEEN HALE (b. 1898)

Born in Scotland. Attended life classes at Manchester Art School, then studied art at Reading University. In 1917 she moved to London, where she attended the Central School of Art and Crafts while designing book jackets and posters and illustrating children's stories. She is most famous for her Orlando books, a series of stories based on the adventures of a large marmalade cat, which she wrote for her own children. Although his adventures were flights of fantasy, the character of Orlando, like that of Jean de Brunhoff's Babar (of which Hale was a great admirer), remains perfectly plausible — in keeping with her belief that fantasy should always have some basis in reality. She was awarded the OBE in 1976.

1 *BOOK:*
ORLANDO BUYS A COTTAGE
by Kathleen Hale

DATE: 1963

2, 3 *BOOK:*
ORLANDO.
THE FRISKY HOUSEWIFE
by Kathleen Hale

DATE: 1956

1

2

3

PETER BLAKE (b. 1932)

*Born in Dartford, UK. Studied at Gravesend
Technical College and School of Art, and
attended the Royal College of Art from 1953-
56. He spent a year studying folk art in
Europe, an experience clearly reflected in his
early work. Other influences have been the
popular Victorian realists and American
Symbolic Realists such as Ben Shahn.
Although a brilliant draughtsman, he was best
known during the 60s for his collage work,
incorporating everyday consumer items,
advertisements, photographs of pin-up girls
and other ephemera, and was very much part
of the British Pop Art movement. His
illustrative work includes* Summer with
Monica *by Roger McGough, several covers for
the Arden* Shakespeare *series published by
Methuen, album sleeves, posters and
magazines. He has held several one-man
exhibitions in London, Europe and Japan,
exhibited with "The Ruralists" in 1981 and is
represented in major public collections
throughout the world.*

1 *RECORD ALBUM COVER:*
SGT PEPPER'S LONELY HEARTS
CLUB BAND

DATE: 1967

2 *PERIODICAL:*
THE TIMES LITERARY
SUPPLEMENT

DATE: 1966

3 *MAGAZINE:*
THE SUNDAY TIMES MAGAZINE

DATE: 1969

1

2

3

PETER MAX (b. 1937)

*Born in Berlin, Germany. Spent his childhood
in Shanghai, where he developed his interest
in Eastern art and philosophy. When he was
12 his family moved to Israel, where he studied
art and astronomy. In the mid-50s his family
took him to New York, where he attended the
Art Students League, the Pratt Institute and
the School of Visual Arts. In 1962 he set up a
design studio with his friend Daly, which over
the next two years won an astonishing 68
awards for excellence in illustration, design
and typography. Max's personal art form,
"Cosmic Art", took its inspiration from nature
as he believed that "it is in nature that the most
beautiful things are to be found". Religion,
mythology and oriental symbolism are all
important components of his designs, which
have come to epitomize the aesthetics of
the 1960s.*

1 *POSTER:*
USA LIBERAL PARTY, NEW YORK

DATE: 1969

2 *POSTER:* NBC TELEVISION

DATE: 1969

3 *POSTER:* TOULOUSE-LAUTREC

DATE: 1967

1

2

DR SEUSS (b. 1904)

Born Theodor Seuss Geisel in Massachusetts, USA. He was educated at Dartmouth College and did a post-graduate year at Oxford University in England. His intention was to become a professor of English Literature. However, after travelling in Europe for a year he returned to America, where he spent 15 years working in advertising. In 1937 he published his first book, And to think that I saw it on Mulberry Street, *and has since published 27 children's books featuring strange creatures of his own design — hybrids of cats, bears and human beings. This strange menagerie has proven to be enduringly popular.*

1, 2 *BOOK:* THE SLEEP BOOK
by Dr Seuss

DATE: 1962

3 *BOOK:* THE FOOT BOOK
by Dr Seuss

DATE: 1968

BRIAN WILDSMITH (b. 1930)

Born in Penistone, UK. After abandoning a promising career in chemistry, he studied at the Barnsley School of Art and then at the Slade School of Fine Art. He became a freelance illustrator at the age of 27 and had two books published in 1959, The Story of Jesus *by Eleanor Graham and* The Daffodil Bird *by Ruth Tomalin. Since then he has written and illustrated nearly 20 books, including* Brian Wildsmith's ABC, *which won the Kate Greenaway Medal in 1962. Within each of his drawings, both black and white and full colour, he uses a wide variety of media and techniques to create a striking array of textures, and his style was extremely influential throughout the 1960s.*

1, 2 *BOOK:*
BRIAN WILDSMITH'S ABC

DATE: 1962

Left foot
Left foot

Right foot
Right

3

216

1

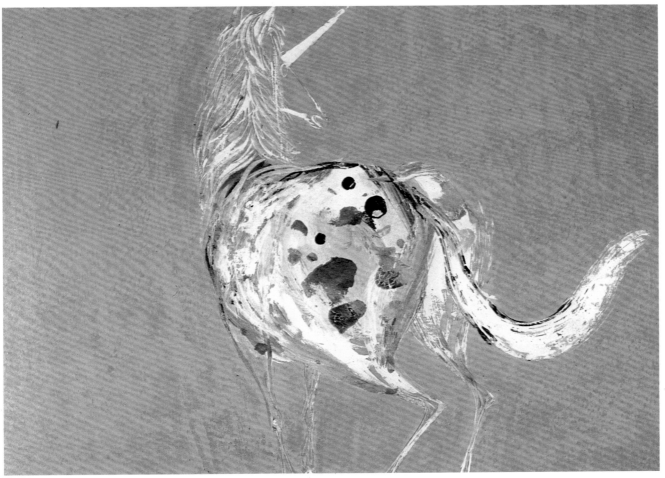

2

1

2

MARTIN SHARP (b. 1942)

Born in Sydney, Australia. He studied at the East Sydney Art School and after graduating in 1963 produced cartoons and graphics for Richard Neville's magazine Oz. *In 1966 these illustrations were published under the title* Martin Sharp Cartoons *and, in the same year, he, Neville and* Oz *moved to London. Over the next three years Sharp's psychedelic, day-glo paintings became icons of underground art and, as well as working prolifically for* Oz, *he produced posters for the Big O poster company and illustrated album covers for The Cream's* Disraeli Gears *and* Wheels of Fire. *In 1969 he returned to Australia and has since concentrated on paintings and posters. In 1972 he published* Artbook, *a collection of his work, which reveals such diverse influences as René Magritte and Vincent van Gogh. In 1988 he exhibited his posters in Brighton, UK, and for the last ten years he has been making a film about the life of Tiny Tim, provisionally titled "Street of Dreams".*

1 *MAGAZINE:* OZ

DATE: 1968

2 *MAGAZINE:* OZ

DATE: 1968

3 *POSTER:* BOB DYLAN

DATE: 1967

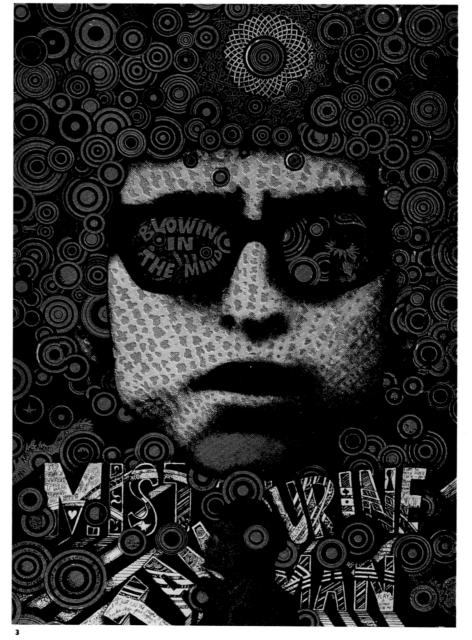

3

VICTOR MOSCOSO (b. 1936)

Born in Spain. Moscoso lives and works in America, where during the 1960s he achieved eminence as an underground artist. His earliest works were a series of posters in 1967 for the Avalon and Fillmore ballrooms in San Francisco, where bands such as the Grateful Dead were playing. In the late 1960s he was a staff artist on Rolling Stone *magazine, then in the 1970s became more involved in comic book illustration. His work appears in* All Stars *(1970), his own book,* Color *(1971), and* Sci-Fi Comics, *which also featured the drawings of Robert Crumb and Gilbert Shelton. His most notable comic work is featured in the* Zap Comix *series, which is still in print. Moscoso's definitively psychedelic style made him popular with underground publications around the world and he was featured heavily in London's* Oz *and* International Times. *His pictures have also appeared in* Playboy *and in advertisements for Levi jeans.*

▌ *COMIC:* ZAP

DATE: c. 1969

JOHN BURNINGHAM (b. 1936)

Born in Farnham, UK. Studied at the Central School of Art. After graduation, he wrote his own stories to get his work published. His first book, Borka: The Adventures of a Goose with no Feathers, *won the Kate Greenaway Medal in 1963, and* Mr Gumpy's Outing *won the medal again in 1970 as well as the Boston Globe* Horn Book *Award for illustration in 1972. Burningham works in full colour using an array of media — india ink, crayons, gouache, cellulose, montage, printer's ink, pastel and photostats. He says of children's illustration: "A beautiful picture is not enough; a mixture of action, detail and atmosphere is important." He lives and works in London.*

1 *POSTER:* LONDON TRANSPORT

DATE: 1963

2 *POSTER:* LONDON TRANSPORT

DATE: c. 1960

3 *BOOK:* MR GUMPY'S OUTING
by John Burningham

DATE: 1970

4 *BOOK:* TROUBLOFF
by John Burningham

DATE: 1964

'All passengers and stores aboard? Right, let go aft. Starboard 30, slow ahead. Set course for Windsor. (sings) Farewell and adieu to you ladies of Staines.'

Lubbers may prefer to have their seamanship done for them, but pilot or passenger, they will find the new London Transport free manual of navigation 'A Day on the River' full of ideas and nautical suggestions. Indent for your copy at any London Transport Enquiry Office, or write to the Public Relations Officer, 55 Broadway, S.W.I.

THIS IS A REPRODUCTION OF A POSTER DESIGNED FOR LONDON TRANSPORT

1

ZOO AHOY

By WATERBUS on the Regent's Canal
Trips hourly from 10 a.m. to 6 p.m. (2 p.m. to 6 p.m. on Sundays) starting from Little Venice. Buses 6, 18 and 187 go to Little Venice. Or by Underground to Warwick Avenue, then a short walk. The starting point is in Delamere Terrace.

By BUS on terra firma
Bus 74 passes the gates. Buses 3, 53 and 276 (Mondays to Saturdays) pass within a short walk of the gates.
By UNDERGROUND
to Camden Town or Baker Street then bus 74.

For Whipsnade take a Green Line Coach
726 (limited stop service) from Baker Street

2

3

4

1

2

3

AL PARKER (b. 1906)

Born in St Louis, USA. He paid his way through art school by playing saxophone in a jazz band. On graduating he worked in a small local studio, then moved to New York in the mid-1930s. He was an immediate success and much emulated by contemporary illustrators. His extraordinary versatility was such that he once illustrated an entire issue of Cosmopolitan *magazine using a different name and style for each story. He is in no way limited by technique and works comfortably in any combination of media. In 1939 he illustrated a mother-daughter cover for* Ladies' Home Journal *which was so popular that he completed a series of 50 of them over the next 12 years. He has won more than 25 Gold Medals for the excellence of his work and was elected to the Society of Illustrators Hall of Fame in 1965.*

1 *MAGAZINE:* WOMAN

DATE: 1960

2 *MAGAZINE:*
SPORTS ILLUSTRATED

DATE: 1964

3 *ADVERTISEMENT:*
AMERICAN AIRLINES

DATE: 1965

221

MICHAEL ENGLISH (b. 1943)

Born in London. Studied at Ealing College of Art. In 1967 he formed a design company, Haphash and the Coloured Coat, with Nigel Waymouth, the co-owner of the cult King's Road shop Granny Takes a Trip. Over the next two years they produced many psychedelic posters advertising underground events in London. English's work also appeared in the counter-culture's foremost magazine International Times. *His paintings, which are definitive of the psychedelic era, were the product of an extraordinarily eclectic style. His influences embraced the Nouveau period of Beardsley and Mucha, Art Deco, Hindu symbolism, Japanese and Islamic decoration, Surrealist imagery and cartoon-style typography. English was also interested in the ephemera of the late 60s, designing T-shirts and sunglasses decorated with the Union Jack. With the arrival of the 70s his work changed dramatically and he abandoned the esoteric in favour of an exploration of the minutiae of urban life through his airbrushed, hyper-realistic illustrations.*

1 *POSTER:*
LIVERPOOL LOVE FESTIVAL

DATE: 1968

2 *POSTER:*
LOVE ME FILM PRODUCTIONS

DATE: 1969

3 *POSTER:*
JIMI HENDRIX CONCERT

DATE: 1968

1

2

3

1   2

3

ROBERT CRUMB (b. 1943)

Born in Philadelphia, USA. He started drawing cartoons as a child and drew comic books with his brother as a teenager. This is when he first created "Fritz the Cat", the cartoon character for which he is most famous and which was made into an X-rated animation film in 1971. In 1962 he moved to Cleveland, Ohio, and, from 1964, started drawing for the underground newspapers Yarrowstalks *and* East Village Other. *In 1966 he moved to San Francisco, where he started the hugely popular* Zap *and* Snatch *comics. His fluid, expressive cartoons, executed in pen and ink, brilliantly reflected the hippy drug culture of the 60s and early 70s, when his "Schuman the Human" and "Mr Natural" characters, and his sexually explicit cartoons, often starring himself as the unlikely victim of sex-starved women, reached the peak of their popularity. Books include* The Snatch Sampler *(1977) and* Head Comix *(1968).*

1 *COMIC:* NOTE
DATE: 1959

2 *COMIC:* ARCADE
DATE: 1962

3 *COMIC:* FRITZ THE CAT
DATE: 1962

1

2

ROBIN JACQUES (b. 1920)

Born in London. Brother of the actress Hattie Jacques, he was educated in Hertfordshire and worked in an advertising agency while submitting illustrations to the Radio Times. *After the war he became a full-time freelance illustrator, his first commissions being Dickens'* Doctor Marigold *(1945) and Cross's* The Angry Planet *(1945). In 1948 he was appointed art editor of* The Strand Magazine *and has contributed to many other magazines, including* The Leader, The Listener, Punch, Vogue, The Sunday Times, Nova *and* The Observer. *His drawings are meticulously detailed and usually executed in line, sometimes with an ink or watercolour wash. He has a particular interest in 19th-century literature and places a great emphasis on research to ensure the accuracy of his drawings.*

1 *MAGAZINE:* THE LEADER
DATE: 1950

2 *MAGAZINE:* THE LEADER
DATE: 1950

3 *MAGAZINE:* THE LEADER
DATE: 1950

4 *BOOK:*
FORTY-TWO STORIES
by Hans Christian Andersen
DATE: 1953

3

4

JOHN GILROY (1898–1985)

Born in Newcastle, UK. Educated at King Edward VI College in Newcastle, he went on to study at the Royal College of Art, London. On returning from a travelling scholarship to Europe, he became a teacher at the Royal College, designing advertising posters in his spare time. He joined the staff of S H Benson Ltd in 1925 and began a long and distinguished career in advertising art. His posters for Guinness beer, stylized but realistic humorous images with accompanying slogans such as the famous "My goodness, my Guinness", were produced prolifically during the 1930s, when new ideas were required continuously. He also contributed illustrations to Radio Times *throughout the 1930s. After World War II, Gilroy concentrated seriously on portrait painting, working on commissions that included portraits of Sir Winston Churchill as well as several members of the British Royal Family.*

1 *ADVERTISEMENT:* GUINNESS BEER

DATE: 1940

2 *ADVERTISEMENT:* GUINNESS BEER

DATE: 1956

3 *ADVERTISEMENT:* GUINNESS BEER

DATE: 1953

BRUCE BOMBERGER (1918–1980)

*Born in California. With the exception of one
year in New York, Bomberger spent his life
and varied career on the West Coast of
America. He started work in an art studio and
at one point had a studio of his own, but
eventually returned to freelancing. He worked
for many different advertising clients, his most
notable work being his wildlife drawings for
the Weyerhaeuser Timber Company. His
drawings also illustrated the stories and the
editorial pages of such magazines as* True,
The Saturday Evening Post,
Cosmopolitan, Good Housekeeping *and*
This Week. *He was at one time President of
the San Francisco Society of Illustrators.*

1 *PAINTING*

DATE: 1962

2 *MAGAZINE:*
THE SATURDAY EVENING POST

DATE: 1954

1

2

I

2

STEVEN SPURRIER (1878–1961)

*Born in London. Studied at London art
schools before taking up a career as a freelance
illustrator. He was particularly associated
with* The London Illustrated News *and
also worked for* The Graphic *and* Radio
Times. *His illustrations were typically line or
line-and-wash, but he was also an
accomplished oil painter and watercolourist
and was elected Royal Academician in 1952.
His lively approach to literary themes is
exemplified by illustrations to Wycherley's*
The Country Wife *(1934), conceived as
scenes on stage with a strong sense of movement
and dramatic lighting. He brought a fresh
character to Dickens' classic* Nicholas
Nickleby *(1940), but was equally attuned to
the work of contemporary novelists, as in* The
Circus is Coming *(1938) by Noel Streatfield
and* The Valley of Song *(1951) by
Elizabeth Goudge.*

I *MAGAZINE:* THE LEADER

DATE: 1950

2 *MAGAZINE:* THE LEADER

DATE: 1950

1

2

ROBERT PEAK (b. 1929)

Born in Denver, Colorado, USA. Studied geology at Wichita State University, then enrolled at the Art Center College of Design in Los Angeles. In 1953 he moved to New York, where he was much in demand due to his ability to work in a broad range of styles using different media and techniques. His first cinema poster was for West Side Story *in 1960, since when he has illustrated posters for many box office successes, including* Camelot, *for which he won a Society of Illustrators gold medal,* Hair, The Missouri Breaks *and* The Last Emperor. *Although he denies having a particular style, he admits to being influenced by Art Nouveau and has a passion for Egon Schiele, Degas, Matisse and the French Impressionists. Clients have included* Life, Look, Esquire, Cosmopolitan, Sports Illustrated *and* Playboy *magazines, Coca Cola, the US Postal Service and a number of major film companies, including MGM and Walt Disney. He has won numerous gold and silver medals, was voted Artist of the Year in 1961 by the Artists Guild of New York, won the Hamilton King Award in 1968 and was elected to the Society of Illustrators Hall of Fame in 1977.*

1 *ADVERTISEMENT:*
NEW YORK WORLD'S FAIR

DATE: 1964

2 *ADVERTISEMENT:*
NEWSWEEK MAGAZINE

DATE: 1964

3 *ADVERTISEMENT:* SS FRANCE

DATE: 1964

3

1

2

3

FRANK BELLAMY (1917—1976)

Born in Kettering, UK. Bellamy was one of the first Englishmen working in comic books to achieve international recognition as an illustrator. In the early 1950s he drew advertising campaigns for The Daily Telegraph, World's Press Agency *and* Ad Weekly *as well as illustrations for* Home Notes, Boy's Own Paper, Men Only *and covers for* Lilliput. *His first comic strip was an advertisement for a toothpaste company and was called* Commando Gibbs v Dragon Decay. *In 1957 he joined the* Eagle *comic and illustrated the life of Winston Churchill in a strip called* The Happy Warrior. *It was the first time that the biography of a living individual had been drawn in this style and it was serialized on the back page. In 1960 he was asked to redesign* Dan Dare *for the front page and in 1962 he created* Heros The Spartan, *which won him the Academy of Comic Book Arts award in America as Best Foreign Comic-Book Artist. He was an immaculate draughtsman whose work had an almost photographic realism. He inked directly onto the art board and coloured in with gouache and waterproof inks, creating artwork that was as perfect as the printed page. In the latter part of his life he gave up comics, but continued to draw a black-and-white newspaper strip called* Garth *until his death in 1976.*

1 *MAGAZINE:* EAGLE

DATE: 1960

2 *MAGAZINE:* EAGLE

DATE: 1960

3 *MAGAZINE:* EAGLE

DATE: 1963

BRIAN LOVE (b. 1942)

Born in London. Studied at Gravesend and Walthamstow Schools of Art and the Royal College of Art. From the mid-60s his obsession with American and British popular culture, and his collection of popular magazines and juvenile literature, became the prime source of reference for his illustration work, much of which attempted to pastiche the colour and compositional arrangement found in such publications. His work as a print maker greatly influenced the way in which he assembled and designed his illustrations. In many cases he produced line-separated artwork which only formed the completed image when printed. His work has appeared in Town, Nova, Radio Times, The Sunday Times, Observer *and* Vogue *magazines and illustrated* The Beatles' Lyrics *in 1968. Even more prolific as a fine artist, he has had one-man exhibitions of his sculptures in Holland and Germany. In 1978 he mounted a touring exhibition entitled "Aerial Drop" — a never-before-seen collection of propaganda leaflets dropped from airplanes. He has also compiled two books on board games,* Play the Game *(1978) and* Great Board Games *(1979).*

1 *MAGAZINE:* RADIO TIMES

DATE: 1969

2 *MAGAZINE:*
THE SUNDAY TIMES MAGAZINE

DATE: 1969

3 *MAGAZINE:*
THE SUNDAY TIMES MAGAZINE

DATE: 1969

4 *AIRBRUSHED BLACK-AND-WHITE PHOTOGRAPH:*
DAVID BAILEY AND MARIE HELVIN
(unpublished)

DATE: 1969

5 *MAGAZINE:*
THE SUNDAY TIMES MAGAZINE

DATE: 1969

6 *MAGAZINE:*
THE SUNDAY TIMES MAGAZINE

DATE: 1968

1

2

3

4

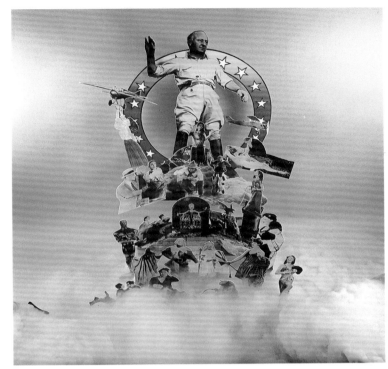

5

6

RICHARD WEIGAND (b. 1942)

Born in London. Trained as a typographer at the London College of Printing and then worked as assistant to Hans Neuberg. In 1965 he became a freelance illustrator and graphic designer and over the next four years worked regularly for magazines such as The Sunday Times *and* Radio Times. *In 1969 he moved to America and from 1970-75 was art director of* Esquire *magazine. He received numerous awards for his work, which he says was never inspired by other illustrators but by the films, pop and montage art of the time. From 1975-79 he was director of the Children's Television Workshop, an educational development of the Sesame Street Muppets. He still lives and works in New York, where he is freelance consultant and planner to the magazine publishing industry.*

I *MAGAZINE:*
THE SUNDAY TIMES MAGAZINE

DATE: 1968

2 *MAGAZINE:*
THE SUNDAY TIMES MAGAZINE

DATE: 1968

ROGER LAW (b. 1941)

Born near Cambridge, UK. Studied at Cambridge School of Art, where he met Peter Fluck, with whom he later formed the partnership responsible for the Spitting Image TV series. After leaving college he worked with Peter Cook on a satirical strip for the Observer, and also drew giant topical cartoons for the walls of Cook's nightclub "The Establishment", where he met Lenny Bruce and other stand-up comics who influenced his later work. In 1963 he joined the art department of The Sunday Times magazine as an illustrator and collaborated with David King on a series of record covers and posters. In 1967 he was a Rockefeller Foundation winner, was artist-in-residence at Reed College, Oregon, for six months and spent the following two years in America. He did fashion drawings and illustration in San Francisco and worked at Push Pin Studios in New York. On his return to England he became features editor of The Sunday Times magazine and in 1975 formed the Luck and Flaw partnership with Peter Fluck.

1 *MAGAZINE:*
THE SUNDAY TIMES MAGAZINE

DATE: c. 1968

2 *MAGAZINE:*
THE SUNDAY TIMES MAGAZINE

DATE: 1969

3 *MAGAZINE:* NOVA

DATE: c. 1967

AUSTIN BRIGGS (1909–1973)

Born in Detroit, Michigan, USA. Studied at the Wicker Art School. He began his art career as assistant to an automobile illustrator, then drew for the Dearborn Independent *before enrolling at the Art Students League in New York. During the Depression he did a variety of jobs, including ghosting the Flash Gordon strip and doing pulp illustrations for* Blue Book *magazine. He had an unlimited repertoire of techniques, sometimes reducing his drawings to the barest line and at other times illustrating in delicate coloured washes. Most prolific at a time when photography was making real inroads into magazine publishing, he specialized in the candid pose, mimicking the camera's ability to freeze the moment, and often seeming to catch his subject unawares. His work appeared in* Collier's, McClure's, Cosmopolitan, Redbook *and* The Saturday Evening Post, *and his advertising clients included Douglas PC Airliners. He was elected to the Society of Illustrators Hall of Fame in 1969.*

I *MAGAZINE:* WOMAN

DATE: 1960

1

2

3

ROBERT FAWCETT (1903—1967)

*Born in London. The son of a keen amateur
artist, he grew up in Canada and New York.
At the age of 19 he returned to London to study
at the Slade School of Fine Art, then in 1924
returned to America and embarked on a career
as a freelance illustrator. His superb
draughtsmanship and compositions quickly
earned him a reputation as one of America's
finest illustrators, and he worked prolifically
on editorial and advertising commissions.
During the 1950s he limited his work to
reportage and in 1958 he wrote and illustrated*
On the Art of Drawing. *He returned to
London in 1960 to paint a series of murals for
the Commonwealth Institute and in 1967 was
elected to the Society of Illustrators Hall of
Fame.*

1 *MAGAZINE:* COLLIER'S

DATE: 1951

2 *MAGAZINE:* COLLIER'S

DATE: 1951

3 *MAGAZINE:*
THE SATURDAY EVENING POST

DATE: 1945

ROWLAND EMETT (b. 1906)

Born in London. Trained at Birmingham College of Arts and Crafts. Emett is known as the latter-day Heath Robinson, both for his graphic work and for his working models of the eccentric machines described in his illustrations. His fascination for railways is seen in twelve books produced between 1943 and 1958, including Engines, Aunties and Others *(1943),* Sidings and Suchlike *(1946) and* Buffer's End *(1949). His figures frequently seem as endearingly antiquated as his machines. He contributed illustrations to* Punch, Life, Vogue *and* Harper's Bazaar, *among others, and created advertising images for Shell and Guinness. He converted antique railway drawings into a full-size, passenger-carrying model for the Festival of Britain in 1951, and produced the Edwardian-style vehicles featured in the 1968 film* Chitty Chitty Bang Bang. *Smaller models have been created for window displays and commercial exhibitions.*

I—4 *BOOK:* BELLS AND GRASS
by Walter De La Mare

DATE: 1941

1

2

3

4

236

ERIC FRASER (b. 1902)

*Born in London. Studied at Westminster
School of Art under Walter Sickert, then at
Goldsmith's School of Art, where he was
influenced by the line draughtsman Edmund
Sullivan and the painter Clive Gardiner. In
1924 he exhibited etchings at the Royal
Academy and from 1930-38 was a fashion
designer for* Harper's Bazaar. *Although
perhaps best remembered for the strong black-
and-white illustrations he produced for the
BBC, and which appeared frequently in the*
Radio Times, *he was also a stained glass
artist and designed murals for the Glasgow
Exhibition in 1938 and the Festival of Britain
in 1951. He taught lithography at Goldsmith's
and graphic design at Camberwell School of
Art and his illustrated books include* English
Legends *(1951),* The Book of a Thousand
and One Nights *(1958) and* Sir William
and the Wolf *(1960).*

1 *MAGAZINE:* RADIO TIMES
DATE: c. 1940
2 *MAGAZINE:* RADIO TIMES
DATE: c. 1940
3 *MAGAZINE:* RADIO TIMES
DATE: c. 1940

OVER THE LAST 150 YEARS, politics and war have created an important field of activity for the illustrator. However, the period since 1970 has been one of relative stability, and the ensuing prosperity in the West has had a subtle but profound effect on artists' lives.

The psychedelic '60s actually ended in about 1972, by which time most of their excesses had been softened by their absorption into mainstream culture. The next style revolution was that of punk rock, which took place about three years later. Its effect was most noticeable in the worlds of fashion and music, but it did make an impact on graphic design and particularly on typography. Its effect on illustration was less noticeable. The '60s had enabled illustrators to develop such a diversity of styles that there was no predominant school for punk aestheticism to assail and therefore no obvious reaction took place.

The main influences on illustration have in fact come from developments within the publishing industry. It is a common belief that book illustration went into decline during the period between the wars and that it has never recovered. This is not entirely true. One has only to look through the examples in this chapter to see that children's book illustration is still booming in the hands of such artists as Helen Oxenbury, Wayne Anderson, Nicola Bayley and Michael Foreman. In fact this market is so healthy that many illustrators, like Maurice Sendak in the USA, have taken to writing their own stories as opposed to reinterpreting the commercial classics. An interesting consequence of this has been the opportunity for artists such as Raymond Briggs to then diversify into animation by selling story rights to a film company.

What has changed is the range of activities within book publishing. The gift book, in the Edwardian sense, has all but disappeared. Modern novels and poetry are rarely illustrated. The craze for coffee-table books has focused on popular education subjects that have been best documented by photography.

However, the book industry as a whole continues to expand and provide a plentiful supply of work in the form of paperback covers and dust jackets. And, perhaps to carve a niche within this market, it seems increasingly common for illustrators to specialize within a literary genre. This is particularly true of science fiction, a field which is now dominated by the styles of artists like Jim Burns, Chris Foss and Peter Jones.

As far as the illustrator is concerned, the magazine business has never been so promising. Prosperitiy creates increased leisure time and with it the proliferation of special interest magazines. These in turn create interesting possibilities for younger artists: as production budgets are often low while a magazine struggles to establish itself, and consequently art departments are prepared to experiment with less proven, but less expensive talent.

Advertising, too, is going from strength to strength, and provides artists with a major source of work. It also encourages a diversity of styles, as the very nature of its business is to differentiate, both practically and aesthetically, one product from another. This has led many illustrators to find work at the agencies and, because advertising is the most plagiaristic of skills, it has proven especially lucrative for artists, like Mick Brownfield in the UK, who can accurately parody bygone styles.

The current diversity of media opportunities has led to a correspondingly wide range of illustration styles. But no real "stars" have emerged. Illustrators, unlike their counterparts of the '20s, are no longer household names. The artist Bernie Fuchs said in his introduction to a book on American illustration that the illustrator today is more like a businessman than the artist of old. But if that's the case, one has to say that business is good. In fact, we may well look back on the '70s and '80s as yet another "golden age" of illustration.

CHAPTER FOUR

1970-1990

ROGER DEAN (b. 1944)

*Born in Kent, UK. Studied industrial design
(furniture) at the Canterbury School of Art
(1961—64), then spent three years at the Royal
College of Art. His first assignment was to
design the seating for "Upstairs" at Ronnie
Scott's jazz club in London. Between 1968
and 1973 he worked prolifically, designing
stage sets, posters, furniture, hotels and office
towers. His record-sleeve designs for the rock
groups Osibisa, Yes, Asia and the Rolling
Stones quickly established him as the foremost
illustrator of record-album covers in Britain.*

*With his brother, Martyn, he formed the
company Dragon's Dream in 1975 to publish
his book* Views, *featuring Roger's fantasy and
science fiction designs for record sleeves. Packed
with hundreds of colour plates, and selling for
the price of a record album, it went straight to
the top of* The Sunday Times *best-seller list
and sold half a million copies world-wide. In
1976 the Deans set up a second company, with
Hubert Schaafsma, to publish books under the
Paper Tiger imprint. In 1979 he became a
director of the Magnetic Storm design
company, specializing in product research and
development.*

1 "RELAYER"
DATE: 1987
2 "DRAMA"
DATE: 1979
3 "PYRAMID"
DATE: 1983
4 "FREYJAS CASTLE"
DATE: 1987
5 "RED DRAGON"
DATE: 1986

4

5

MAURICE SENDAK (b. 1928)

Born in Brooklyn, New York. Studied at the Art Students League. In 1952 he illustrated A Hole is to Dig *by Ruth Krauss. It was a huge success, and revolutionary in its day because there was no storyline; the book consisted of a series of illustrated children's definitions, such as "dogs are to kiss people", and so on. Although Sendak's illustrations appeared in many books by other authors, his most significant books were those he wrote himself, including* Where the Wild Things Are *(1962), which won both the Hans Christian Andersen and the Caldecott awards,* In the Night Kitchen *(1970) and* Higglety Pigglety Pop! *(1967), which was written in dedication to his dog, Julie, who had died shortly before. Increasingly Sendak has begun to link his art to music. He co-wrote, with Carole King, an animated TV musical,* Really Rosie, *and wrote the libretto and designed the sets for an opera version of* Where the Wild Things Are *in 1979.*

1, 2 *BOOK:*
WHERE THE WILD THINGS ARE
by Maurice Sendak

DATE: 1962

3 *BOOK:* IN THE NIGHT KITCHEN
by Maurice Sendak

DATE: 1970

1

2

3

NICOLA BAYLEY (b. 1949)

Born in Singapore. Studied graphic design at Saint Martin's School of Art and then entered the Royal College of Art, where she studied illustration and developed a style that is rich in detail and colour and which uses a fine stippling technique to create a range of distinctive textures. Her illustrations of old nursery rhymes were spotted by a publisher in her diploma show and were later published in a book, One Old Oxford Ox *(1976). She followed this with* Nicola Bayley's Book of Nursery Rhymes *and Richard Adams'* The Tyger Voyage *(both 1976), and* The Patchwork Cat *(1981). All were extremely successful and have been translated into seven languages. She lives in London and works in Arthur Rackham's old studio.*

1, 2 *BOOK:* ONE OLD OXFORD OX
by Nicola Bayley

DATE: 1977

3, 4 *BOOK:*
THE TYGER VOYAGE
by Nicola Bayley & Richard Adams

DATE: 1976

QUENTIN BLAKE (b. 1932)

Born in Sidcup, UK. Studied at Downing College, Cambridge, London University and Chelsea College of Art. He began drawing for Punch *while still at school, and after leaving university also became a regular cover artist for* The Spectator *and designed book jackets for Penguin Books. His first illustrations for children's books appeared in 1960, since when he has illustrated over 150 books, most of them for children, and has had extended collaborations with Roald Dahl, Russell Hoban, Joan Aiken, Michael Rosen and John Yeoman. His* How Tom Beat Captain Najork and his Hired Sportsmen *was joint winner of the Whitbread Award (1974) and* Mister Magnolia *won the Kate Greenaway Medal (1980). He is now a visiting professor at the Royal College of Art, of which he is a Senior Fellow, and where he was Head of Illustration between 1978 and 1986. He was awarded the OBE in 1988.*

1 *BOOK:* RUMBELOW'S DANCE
by John Yeoman

DATE: 1982

2 *MAGAZINE:* PUNCH

DATE: 1980

3 *BOOK:*
A FEAST OF TRUE FANDANGLES
by Patrick Campbell

DATE: 1979

4 *BOOK:* THE BIRDS
by Aristophanes

DATE: 1971

5 *BOOK:*
THE HISTORY OF TOM THUMB

DATE: 1979

2

3

4

5

Nobody knew of their dancing, nobody had ever heard of it or imagined such a thing, and the tigers held their tongues. Silently prowling in their stripes they hunted, unseen they roared and started sudden echoes. They knew they would be hunted down, they knew that every season some of them would die by a bullet from the Rajah's monogrammed gold-mounted jewelled tiger guns. They were primitive and patient and they accepted their lot.

DAVID GENTLEMAN (b. 1930)

Born in London. Studied at St Albans School of Art and the Royal College of Art, where he taught for two years. Since 1955 he has concentrated on his own work, which has included lithography, wood-engraving, graphic design and watercolour painting, and ranges in scale from postage stamps to the platform-length murals on the Underground at Charing Cross station in London. Publishing clients include Penguin Books, Cambridge University Press, Limited Editions Club of New York, Cape and Weidenfeld. He has produced several books of his own, including David Gentleman's Britain *(1982),* David Gentleman's London *(1985),* David Gentleman's Coastline *(1988),* A Special Relationship *(1987) and, with Russell Hoban,* The Dancing Tigers *(1979). He has also written and illustrated several children's books and one book on design.*

1 *BOOK:*
A MIDSUMMER NIGHT'S DREAM
by William Shakespeare

DATE: 1975

2 *BOOK:* HENRY VIII
by William Shakespeare

DATE: 1975

3 *BOOK:* THE DANCING TIGERS
by David Gentleman & Russell Hoban

DATE: 1979

1

2

3

1

2

BRUCE PENNINGTON (b. 1944)

Born in Somerset, UK. Studied at Beckenham and Ravensbourne Schools of Art in Kent. After graduating in 1964 he worked for two years as a commercial artist before becoming a freelance illustrator in 1967, entering the science fiction field with his cover design for Robert Heinlein's Stranger in a Strange Land. *This marked a turning point in his career and, finding science-fiction an excellent medium through which to express his imaginative ideas, he went on to produce covers for several Ray Bradbury novels for Corgi Books. Many of his works were reproduced in* Science Fiction Monthly.

1-3 *BOOK:* ESCHATUS
by Bruce Pennington

DATE: 1977

PETER ANDREW JONES (b. 1951)

Born in London. Studied at Saint Martin's School of Art, where, inspired by the novels of Isaac Asimov and Larry Niven, he became interested in science fiction imagery. His freelance career took off while he was still at college, with some commissions for Puffin Books. In 1979 he designed a book, Solar Wind, *with Roger and Martyn Dean. In the same year, Solar Wind Ltd was formed to market his career, and he branched out into film, TV and video productions. In 1982 he launched a highly successful series of* Fighting Fantasy *games books for Puffin. He has also designed news title sequences, backdrops and inserts for BBC Television, and has exhibited in England, France and Japan.*

1 *BOOK:*
THE QUEST OF THE DNA
COWBOYS
by Mick Farren

DATE: 1975

2 *BOOK:*
THE COMPLETE ENCHANTER
by L Sprague de Camp and Fletcher Pratt

DATE: 1979

JEAN-MICHEL FOLON (b. 1934)

*Born in Brussels, Belgium. Initially studied
architecture, but abandoned it in favour of
becoming an illustrator. Since the mid-60s he
has produced a vast body of work and his
wistful, poetic watercolours, particularly those
featuring his "blue man", have appeared in
many media. He has produced advertising
posters for Olivetti, film posters for Woody
Allen, and record covers for Michele
Colombier and Steve Kahn; illustrated the
works of Kafka and Lewis Carroll (1973),
and the short stories of Jorge-Luis Borges
(1974); created frescoes for the Belgian metro
and the London Underground; designed
theatre scenery for the operas of Frank Martin
and Puccini; and produced animated films for
Cadbury's chocolate in the UK and title
sequences for French TV. In addition to all this,
he has held one-man shows around the world.*

1 *POSTER:*
AMNESTY INTERNATIONAL

DATE: 1977

2 *POSTER*

DATE: 1973

3 *POSTER*

DATE: 1977

4 *EXHIBITION POSTER*

DATE: 1977

5 *SOURCE:* NOT KNOWN

DATE: NOT KNOWN

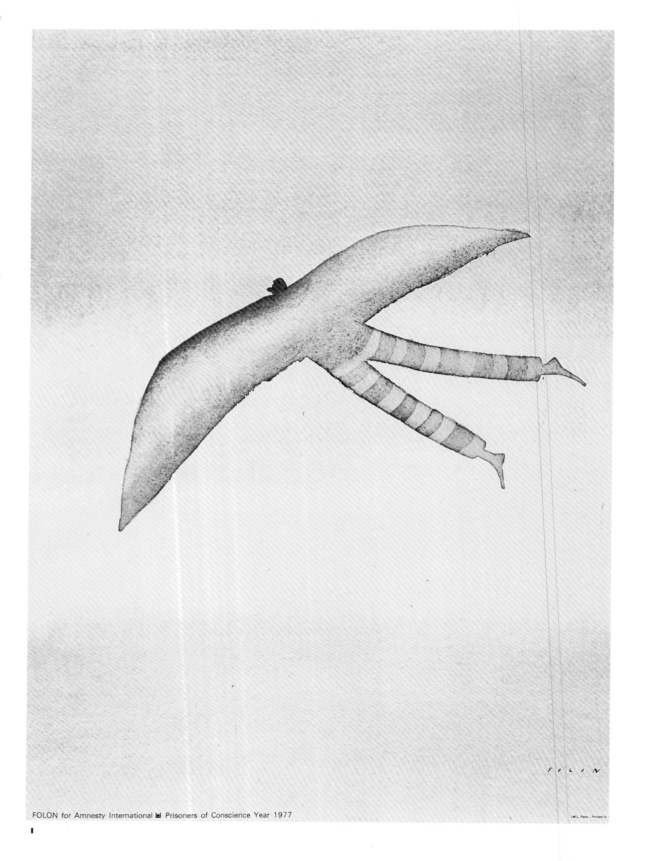

FOLON for Amnesty International ⚫ Prisoners of Conscience Year 1977

I.M.L. Paris - Printed in

1

2

3

4

5

JAN PIENKOWSKI (b. 1936)

Born in Warsaw, Poland. He read English and the Classics at Cambridge and in 1961 was a co-founder of Gallery Five, a greetings card company through which many of his books have been published. In 1967 he illustrated Jessie Townsend's Annie, Bridget and Charlie *and in 1968 formed a collaboration with Joan Aiken which led three years later to the publication of* The Kingdom Under The Sea and Other Stories *(1972), which won the Kate Greenaway Medal. Since 1972 he has produced the* Meg and Mog *series, featuring simplified drawings using strong, flat colours. More recently he has concentrated on highly elaborate pop-up books such as* Haunted House *(1979), a masterpiece of paper engineering which won him the Kate Greenaway Medal for the second time.*

1, 2 *BOOK:* HAUNTED HOUSE
by Jan Pienkowski

DATE: 1979

Do you think it's all imagination? Doctor...?   DOCTOR, WHERE ARE YOU...?

1

I can't seem to settle down. In fact I can't   sit still for two minutes.

2

1

2

3

4

5

TOMI UNGERER (b. 1931)

Born in Strasbourg, France. Spent his early adulthood travelling and doing odd jobs, including a brief stint as a camel-rider with the Sahara Police Force. At the age of 24 he taught himself to draw and paint, and in 1957 moved to New York and established himself as a freelance illustrator. He was immediately successful and his exquisite pen and ink drawings with coloured washes appeared in Life, Esquire, McCalls, The New York Times *and in many advertising campaigns. At the same time he was writing and illustrating his own stories and published* The Mellops Go Diving for Treasure *(1957),* The Mellops Go Flying *(1957) and* Emile *(1960). He won the New York Society of Illustrators Gold Medal in 1960 and the New York Times Best Book of the Year in 1971. Since then he has illustrated many books, including* I am Papa Snap and these are my favourite no-such stories *(1973),* Moon Man *(1980) and* The Hat *(1986).*

I, 2 *BOOK:* THE HAT	
DATE: 1986	
3 *CALENDAR DESIGN FOR* NIXDORF COMPUTERS	
DATE: 1979	
4 *POSTER:* "THE ELECTRIC CIRCUS"	
DATE: 1973	
5 *CALENDAR DESIGN FOR* REGENSDORF	
DATE: 1979	

BERNARD D'ANDREA (b. 1923)

Born in Buffalo, New York. During World War II he spent three years as a War Artist attached to the Quatermaster Corps and the Office of Strategic Services. He began his career as an illustrator in New York in 1950. His first major commission was for The Saturday Evening Post *and between 1950 and 1970 he also illustrated for* Good Housekeeping, Cosmopolitan, Ladies' Home Journal, *and* Woman's Home Companion, *as well as a number of advertising clients. Since 1970 he has concentrated more on book illustration and has worked on historical subjects for the National Geographic Society of Washington DC. He has held several one-man exhibitions and is a member of the New York Society of Illustrators.*

I *MAGAZINE:* BOY'S LIFE

DATE: 1973

2 *BOOK:*
THE MAN WHO MADE
THE BEATLES

DATE: 1976

3 *MAGAZINE:*
GOOD HOUSEKEEPING

DATE: 1976

4 *MAGAZINE:* REDBOOK

DATE: 1976

1

2

3

4

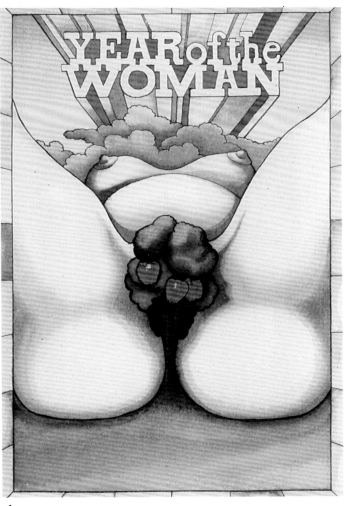

JACQUI MORGAN (b. 1939)

Born in New York. Trained at the Pratt Institute and at Hunter College. She worked briefly as a textile designer, then spent a year in Europe. On her return to America in 1963, she embarked on a career of freelance illustration. Her style, which she describes then as being one of "anthropomorphic double-images", was perfectly suited to the psychedelic period of the mid to late 60s, and after the publication of her poster for the "Electric Circus" she received many commissions from magazines and advertising clients. Using concentrated watercolour, ink and coloured pencils on watercolour paper, she produced images that were surreal, graphic and intensely colourful. She is now one of the foremost watercolourists working in America, has exhibited in New York, West Germany, Japan and the UK and published Watercolour for Illustration *in 1986.*

1 *ADVERTISEMENT:*
SWEDISH TANNING PRODUCT

DATE: 1970

2 *MAGAZINE COVER:*
SUNDAY MAGAZINE

DATE: 1971

3 *RECORD ALBUM COVER:*
CHOPIN

DATE: c. 1970

4 *POSTER:*
"YEAR OF THE WOMAN"

DATE: 1971

1

2

WAYNE ANDERSON (b. 1946)

Born in Leicester, UK. Studied at Leicester College of Art and then pursued a freelance career in London, illustrating album covers, greetings cards and Clement Freud's cookery column in the Daily Telegraph. *After marriage and the birth of his first child he returned to Leicester and concentrated on finely detailed crayon and pencil drawings of animals. His first book,* Ratsmagic *(1976), was a great success and others quickly followed, including* Magic Circus, Mouse's Tale *and a collection of short stories,* The Magic Inkstand, *written by Heinrich Seidle. His one adult book,* Flight of Dragons, *written by Peter Dickenson, was animated into a full-length feature film and shown on British and American television.*

1—3 *BOOK:* RATSMAGIC
by Wayne Anderson

DATE: 1976

3

1

2

Plate 20

3

ALAN ALDRIDGE (b. 1943)

Born in Aylesbury, UK. He left Romford Technical College at 15 and drifted through a variety of jobs, including actor, insurance clerk, barrow boy and stall holder in a London market. At the age of 20 he started to draw and took an evening class in graphic art. Success followed very quickly and soon his work was seen on book covers, album sleeves, posters and in magazines such as Harper's, Nova *and* The Sunday Times. *Within the world of music he was a celebrity artist and received many commissions from leading rock bands and his work appeared frequently in* Melody Maker. *In 1966 he became art director of Penguin Books and then set up his own studio in 1968. The following year he edited and contributed illustrations to both volumes of* The Beatles Illustrated Lyrics *(1969). To the psychedelic art of the 1960s Aldridge brought exquisite draughtsmanship and the innovative use of the airbrush to control the subtle gradation of tone and colour. And although his work was the epitome of the style and aesthetics of the time, it found a new audience when the decade was over. In 1974 he won the Children's Book of the Year Award for* The Butterfly Ball *(1973). He now works freelance in London and has recently been designing animated films.*

1—3 *BOOK:* THE BUTTERFLY BALL
by Alan Aldridge & William Plomer

DATE: 1973

1

PAUL LEITH (b. 1946)

*Born in South Shields, UK. He studied
commercial art at Sunderland Art College
(1961—65) and attended the London College
of Printing in 1969 before going on to study
illustration at the Royal College of Art (1970—
73). Magazine clients include* Vogue, The
Sunday Times, Observer, Company *and*
She, *and he has illustrated books for Penguin,
Futura, Octopus, Pan/Picador and Mitchell
Beazley. Advertising clients include retailers
Liberty, Next and The Body Shop, Royal
Bank of Scotland, Barclays Bank and the
construction company Costain. He exhibited in
the 1983, 1984 (when he won first prize) and
1985 Benson and Hedges Gold Awards
exhibitions. An admirer of the Bauhaus and
Russian art, Leith favours a direct, no-
nonsense approach to his art. He works mainly
with stencils and acrylic paint.*

I "TIME PASSING"
(Benson and Hedges Gold Awards)

DATE: 1984

2 "RELEASING ENERGY"
(Benson and Hedges Gold Awards)

DATE: 1985

2

1

2

"TEA LEAVES"   ©Barbara Nessim 1-89

3

BARBARA NESSIM (b. 1939)

Born in New York. Studied at the Pratt Institute and the Pratt Graphic Art Centre in New York, graduating in 1960. After a brief spell as a textile designer, she returned to her childhood ambition to be an artist after befriending Robert Weaver, who gave her individual tuition and the encouragement to enter her work in the Society of Illustrators show in 1960. Since then she has received over 200 awards for excellence in fine art and illustration. She has illustrated album covers and calendars and for numerous magazines, including Show, New York Magazine, Audience, Ms, Rolling Stone, The Boston Globe, Newsweek *and* Time. *She has taken part in exhibitions all over the world and her work is represented at the Museum of Modern Art in New York, the Smithsonian Institution in Washington and Lund Kunsthall Lund in Sweden. She teaches at the School of Visual Art, the Fashion Institute of Technology and the Pratt Institute in New York. Nessim employs many different expressive media in her work, including computer graphics.*

1 *MAGAZINE:* V MAGAZINE

DATE: 1988

2 *PAINTING:* WOMAN SITTING

DATE: 1987

3 *PAINTING:* TEA LEAVES

DATE: 1989

1

2

DAVID AND RENEE STREET
(b. 1957 and 1954)

*Renee Gettier was born in Baltimore, USA,
and studied art at Towson State University
before transferring to Maryland Institute,
College of Fine Art. After graduating she
worked as an illustrator's assistant for a year
before turning freelance and starting
Streetworks Studio with David Street. At
various times her work has been selected as
among the best of the year by* Graphis, Print
Magazine, The Illustrators Club *and the Art
Directors Club of Metropolitan Washington.
Clients include* The Washington Post,
Psychology Today, 321 Contact,
McDonald's *hamburger chain and* CBS
Records. *David Street was born in
Washington, USA. He studied architecture at
Virginia Polytechnic and State University
before transferring to Maryland Institute,
College of Fine Art. After starting work as a
graphic designer he joined Renee as a freelance
illustrator. Clients include* The Boston
Globe *and* National Wildlife Magazine.
*He became President of the Illustrators Club of
Washington in 1987.*

1 *CHILDREN'S NEWSPAPER:*
PENNYWHISTLE PRESS

DATE: 1988

2 *MAGAZINE:* SCIENCE '86

DATE: 1986

3 *NEWSPAPER:*
THE WASHINGTON POST

DATE: 1985

4 *CHRISTMAS CARD*

DATE: 1987

5 *NEWSPAPER:*
THE BALTIMORE SUN

DATE: 1988

5

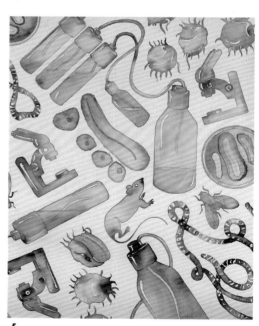

3

1	*POSTER*
	DATE: 1983
2	*MAGAZINE:* PUBLIC CITIZEN
	DATE: 1986
3	*POSTER*
	DATE: 1983
4	*MAGAZINE:* THE SCIENTIST
	DATE: 1988

BILL NELSON (b. 1946)

*Born in Richmond, Virginia, USA. Graduated
from the Richmond Professional Institute in
1970 with a BFA in Communication Art and
Design, and began work as a newspaper
illustrator on* The Richmond Mercury
*before setting up his own studio. His work,
which has been described as "quiet elegance in
coloured pencil", has appeared in* Newsweek,
New Times, The Washington Post
Magazine *and* Time Life *records. He has
won two gold medals from the Art Directors
Club of New York and two silver medals from
the Society of Illustrators, who in 1983
sponsored a travelling exhibition of his work to
Europe and Japan. He has lectured at a
number of art schools throughout the USA and
taught at The Virginia Commonwealth
University's School of the Arts for two years.*

1 *BOOK:*
FINISHING THE HAT.
"TRENCH COAT"

DATE: 1986

2 *RECORD ALBUM COVER:*
MAHLER'S SYMPHONY FOR
CHILDREN

DATE: 1988

3 "AIN'T MISBEHAVIN'"
(unpublished)

DATE: 1988

1

1

2

3

RICHARD ADAMS (b. 1960)

Born in Hampshire, UK. Studied graphic design at Leicester Polytechnic, specializing in illustration. He has won several Benson and Hedges Gold Awards prizes, including second prizes in 1983 and 1984 and first prize in 1986, and was highly commended in 1987. He also won first prize in the 1986 Reader's Digest Young Illustrators Awards. Clients include Cosmopolitan *and* The Listener *magazines, Penguin Books, The Royal Academy of Arts, BBC World Service and a number of advertising clients. He has taken part in several group exhibitions and his work is on permanent show at the Portal Gallery in London and the David Adamson Gallery in Washington. Adams prefers to work in chalk pastel, for its good tonal quality, strong colours and speed, and cites his influence as British naive art and the work of Stanley Spencer.*

I "THE JOURNEY"
(non-commissioned)

DATE: 1987

2 "THE FLORIST"
(non-commissioned)

DATE: 1989

3 "THE SHELL HOUSE AND SUN FISH"
(non-commissioned)

DATE: 1989

DAVE CALVER (b. 1954)

Born in Rochester, New York. He graduated from Rhode Island School of Design in 1976 and immediately established himself as a freelance illustrator. His first commissions were from GQ, Psychology Today *and* New York *magazine. Initially influenced by George Grosz and the films of Fritz Lang, he works in coloured pencil and wryly observes that it is the elegance of his style that has led to his recent popularity with the publishers of murder mystery fiction. As well as illustrating book jackets he contributes regularly to* Vogue *and* Vanity Fair *and has worked for such advertising clients as Mobil, TWA and United Airlines.*

1 *BOOK JACKET:*
SEDUCTION BY LIGHT

DATE: 1988

2 *MAGAZINE:* PLAYBOY

DATE: 1986

3 *POSTER:*
21ST ANNUAL COMPETITION,
SOCIETY OF PUBLICATION
DESIGNERS

DATE: 1986

1

2

3

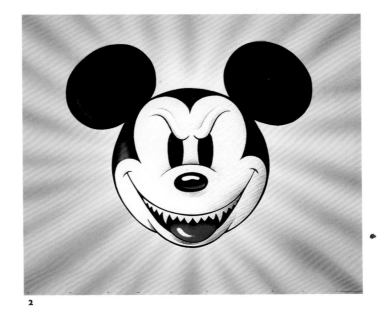

1

2

3

MICK BROWNFIELD (b. 1947)

Born in London. Trained at Hornsey College of Art and has worked as a freelance illustrator since 1973. It is difficult to characterize his work as he is not only prolific but extraordinarily versatile and has on many occasions been commissioned to parody the work of other artists, an example being his drawing for Heineken beer in the style of John Gilroy's poster for Guinness. His work has regularly appeared in the Design and Art Direction Annual, European Illustration, Association of Illustrators *exhibitions and* The One Show Annual *(New York). He has exhibited at several art galleries, including the Pompidou Centre in Paris, and has held a one-man show in Hamburg, West Germany, entitled "Art for Commerce". Advertising and editorial clients include* The Sunday Times *and* Marie Claire *magazines, Guinness, Heineken, Walt Disney and Handmade Films.*

1 *MAGAZINE:*
THE SUNDAY TIMES

DATE: 1987

2 *MAGAZINE:* THE LISTENER

DATE: 1984

3 *ADVERTISEMENT:*
(*unpublished*)

DATE: 1986

4 *MAGAZINE:*
MARIE FRANCE

DATE: 1983

5 *MAGAZINE:*
THE LISTENER

DATE: 1986

4

5

FLUCK AND LAW

Roger Law (b. 1941, see also page 233) and Peter Fluck (b. 1941) met in 1957 as students at Cambridge School of Art, where they co-art directed the Cambridge University magazine Granta *and were inspired by the example of their tutor, Paul Hogarth, "a man doing something he really liked* and *making a living". After graduating in 1963, Fluck worked as a freelance cartoonist for numerous magazines, including* New Society, New Statesman, The Economist *and the* Radio Times, *as well as designing costumes for the Royal Ballet. In 1975 the Luck and Flaw partnership was formed and produced caricature models for photography for several magazines and newspapers, illustrated Dickens'* A Christmas Carol *(1979) and Stevenson's* Treasure Island *(1986) and designed a range of ceramic caricature tableware. The* Spitting Image *TV series, a satirical show starring cruelly accurate caricature puppets of politicians, celebrities and members of the Royal Family, became an instant success in 1984 and led to numerous spin-offs, including books, pop songs and advertising commissions.*

1—6 *TV SERIES:* SPITTING IMAGE

1 THE QUEEN *(1984)*

2 PRINCE CHARLES *(1984)*

3 FRANK BRUNO *(1985)*

4 MARGARET THATCHER *(1984)*

5 P W BOTHA *(1986)*

6 MICHAEL JACKSON *(1984)*

1

2

3

4

5

6

PHILIP CASTLE (b. 1942)

Born in Huddersfield, UK. Trained at Huddersfield School of Art and the Royal College. While still a student he received his first commissions, in 1965, from The Sunday Times *and* Vogue *magazines and in 1967 he was represented in an exhibition of five illustrators at the Time-Life Gallery. Since then he has designed a number of film posters, including those for* Clockwork Orange, The Boyfriend *and* Full Metal Jacket, *and worked on the 1973 Pirelli Calendar with Allen Jones. Castle has become one of the definitive artists of the hyper-realistic airbrush style. He has exhibited in San Francisco and at the Thumb Gallery and Francis Kyle Gallery in London. Magazine clients include* Elle, Marie Claire, Stern, Jasmin, Playboy *and* Time. *Advertising clients include Heineken, Fiat, Ford, Air Canada and Volkswagen. He has produced two books:* Airflow *(1980) and* Airshow *(1989).*

1 *FILM POSTER:*
CLOCKWORK ORANGE

DATE: 1971

2 *POSTCARD:* "TRULY TRIONIC"

DATE: 1978

3 "PATRICK LIDSEY AIRFORCE"
(private commission)

DATE: 1983

GUY BILLOUT (b. 1941)

Born in Decize, France. Studied at the Ecole des Arts Appliqués in Beaune, Burgundy. In 1969 he moved to New York, where he joined an evening art class run by Milton Glaser. This led to his entire portfolio being reprinted in New York Magazine, of which Glaser was then editor. The idea for his first children's book, Bus Number 24 *(1972), a picture story without words, came from a story by Heinrich Hoffman which he came across in an old German book. Since then he has produced several books for children and adults, four of which were chosen by* The New York Times *for their list of ten best-illustrated children's books (1973, '79, '81 and '82). He has also illustrated for* Atlantic, New Republic, Time, Vogue, Playboy *and* Rolling Stone *magazines. Billout has received three gold and two silver medals from the Society of Illustrators, was selected as Illustrator of the Year for the All-Star Creative Team in* Adweek Creativity *(1986) and won first prize in an international contest to design a poster for the World Fair of 1992 in Seville, Spain. His intriguing, meticulously airbrushed images are influenced by Japanese woodblocks and by the flat tones of Hergé, creator of the "Tintin" comic strip.*

1 *MAGAZINE:*
ATLANTIC MONTHLY

DATE: 1986

2 *MAGAZINE:*
ATLANTIC MONTHLY

DATE: 1988

3 *MAGAZINE:*
ATLANTIC MONTHLY

DATE: 1987

4 *MAGAZINE:*
CORPORATE MAGAZINE

DATE: 1987

1

2

3

4

GLYNN BOYD HARTE (b. 1948)

Born in Rochdale, UK. Trained at Rochdale School of Art, Saint Martin's and the Royal College of Art. After graduating he taught at Cambridge School of Art and over the next ten years divided his time between teaching and freelance illustration for various publications, including the Radio Times, *for whom he worked mostly in black and white. He also undertook private commissions and illustrated a letterheading for the playwright Tom Stoppard, who owns several of his paintings. His early work in coloured pencils shows the influence of David Hockney, but his mature paintings are instantly recognizable as being in his own highly individual style. He has illustrated several books, including* Glynn Boyd Harte's Venice *(1988) and is currently working on a book about France. He has exhibited at the Thumb and Francis Kyle galleries and is represented by the Albemarle Gallery in London.*

1 "FOOD STILL LIFE"

DATE: NOT KNOWN

2 *PROMOTIONAL BROCHURE: FONTANA BOOKS*

DATE: 1983

3 *SELF-PROMOTIONAL POSTER*

DATE: 1985

ANDRZEJ DUDZINSKI (b. 1945)

Born in Sopot, Poland. Initially studied architecture at Gdansk Polytechnic, but transferred after two years to the State College of Art, where he studied interior design and printmaking. He then studied poster design and painting at the Academy of Fine Art. He moved to New York in 1977, since when his work has appeared in various magazines and newspapers in Europe and the USA, including The Boston Globe, The New York Times, Newsweek, Playboy, Rolling Stone, Vogue, Vanity Fair, Time, Elle, Tatler *and* The Daily News. *He has exhibited at the National Arts Club in New York, the Dubois Gallery in Pennsylvania, the Atrium in Connecticut and at the National Theatre in London. He currently teaches at Parsons School of Design in New York.*

1 *MAGAZINE:* THE DAILY NEWS
DATE: 1986

2 *POSTER:* SPECTATOR, XIII
DATE: 1983

3 *POSTER*
DATE: 1986

1

2

3

1   **2**

3

CHLOE CHEESE (b. 1952)

*Born in London. Studied at Cambridge School
of Art and the Royal College of Art. Her first
illustrations were for The Sunday Times.
Since then she has worked for Habitat stores,
Walker Books and a number of advertising
clients, and contributed to The Spectator
and A La Carte. She has recently designed a
series of posters for the Seibu department store
in Japan. She won the Lloyds Printmakers
Prize in 1981 and in 1985 her work was
represented in a British Council exhibition
entitled "From Caxton to Chlöe".*

1 *MAGAZINE:* THE SUNDAY TIMES

DATE: 1981

2 *BOOK:*
SPECTATOR BOOK OF TRAVEL
WRITING

DATE: 1988

3 *MAGAZINE:* OBSERVER

DATE: 1985

1

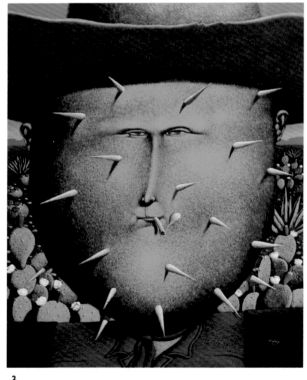

2

3

4

TOM CURRY (b. 1945)

Born in Texas, USA. Studied at North Texas State University in Denton, where he majored in advertising art in 1968. After a short period working as a production artist and designer for an advertising agency in Dallas, he was drafted by the US Army and stationed in Germany, where he developed an interest in the fine arts. On his return to the USA he studied painting and drawing at East Texas State University and became a commercial artist in 1972. After a brief spell working as art director at the University of Texas he became a freelance illustrator. As well as being commissioned by various advertising agencies, his work appeared in such publications as Texas Monthly, Houston City *and* D Magazine. *In 1979 he co-founded the design and illustration group Sagebrush Studio and formed Curry and Associates with two partners in 1983.*

I *MAGAZINE:* ATLANTIC MONTHLY

DATE: 1986

---

2 *MAGAZINE:* TEXAS MONTHLY

DATE: 1985

---

3 *MAGAZINE:* VIDEO MAGAZINE

DATE: 1986

---

4 *ILLUSTRATION:* FOR ADVANCED GRAPHIC SYSTEMS CO.

DATE: 1987

1

2

CHRIS FOSS (b. 1946)

Born in Devon, UK. As a child he loved to build models of steam engines and had a fascination for colour, speed and technology. While studying architecture at Cambridge University, he had a sci-fi comic strip published in Penthouse *magazine. In 1970 one of his paintings appeared in* Nova *and this led to other commissions, most notably for Arthur C Clarke's* Coming of the Space Age. *The following three years saw Foss establish himself as one of the most prolific and sought-after science-fiction illustrators, with Isaac Asimov personally requesting that Foss should illustrate his* Foundation Series *(1973). Foss produces his highly detailed and colourful paintings in airbrush and his revolutionary view of technology and transport in the future has influenced the entire genre. He has also worked on three films, Richard Donner's* Superman *(1978) and Ridley Scott's* Alien *(1979) as well as Jodorowski's never-completed version of* Dune.

1 *BOOK:* WE CAN BUILD YOU
by P K Dick

DATE: 1986

2 *BOOK:* ASTEROID COLLISION

DATE: 1987

3 *BOOK:* STAR KING
by Jack Vance

DATE: 1988

3

BERNIE FUCHS (b. 1933)

Born in O'Fallon, Illinois, USA. Studied at the Washington University School of Fine Arts in St Louis, Missouri. He began his career in 1957 in Detroit, Michigan, working on automobile accounts. Later he moved to New York, where he illustrated for The Saturday Evening Post, The New Yorker *and* Sports Illustrated, *among others. His exquisite illustrations, which show the influence of the French Impressionists, ensured his early success as both an illustrator and a painter. At the age of only 30 he was named Artist of the Year by the Artists Guild of New York and in the same year was commissioned to paint the official portrait of President Kennedy. In 1975 he was the youngest artist ever to be elected to the Illustrators Hall of Fame, since when he has won the Hamilton King Award and many gold and silver medals from the Society of Illustrators. In 1981 he was commissioned to paint the portraits of President and Mrs Reagan. He has exhibited his work in New York, Chicago, Atlanta, New Orleans, England, Russia and Japan.*

1 *RECORD ALBUM COVER:* TIME LIFE RECORDS	
DATE: 1980	
2 *POSTER:* THE BIRTH DEFECTS FOUNDATION	
DATE: 1988	
3 *MAGAZINE:* TV GUIDE	
DATE: NOT KNOWN	

ROBERT GROSSMAN (b. 1940)

Born in New York. He was encouraged to draw as a child and attended Saturday morning art classes at the Museum of Modern Art in New York. He studied art at Yale, under Joseph Alber, and contributed illustrations to the college magazine, The Yale Record. *He also edited a magazine called* Yew Norker *— a spoof on* New Yorker *magazine — which, after he graduated in 1961, led to his first job as a cartoon editor. Since becoming a freelance illustrator and cartoonist in 1965 he has illustrated for a number of magazines, including* Time, Newsweek, Esquire *and* Forbes. *He also designed the publicity poster for the film* Airplane, *taught at Syracuse University in New York and illustrated for a number of advertising clients.*

1 *MAGAZINE:*
THE NEW REPUBLIC

DATE: 1988

2 *MAGAZINE:* FORBES

DATE: 1988

3 *MAGAZINE:* FORBES

DATE: 1988

4 *NEWSPAPER:*
PENNSYLVANIA GAZETTE

DATE: 1988

1

2

3

4

1

2

3

BRIAN GRIMWOOD (b. 1948)

Born in Beckenham, UK. Studied at Bromley Technical High School, where he was able to study typography, life drawing and graphics before the age of 16. He worked in an advertising studio until he saw a Push Pin Studios exhibition in 1968, which inspired him to become a freelance illustrator. Striving to come up with "novel images that will become classics", his influences range from George Grosz to Japanese packaging and from Picasso to Seymour Chwast, whom he met when he visited New York in 1974. He has worked for all the major magazines and publications in the UK, Europe and the USA, and for top advertising agencies all over the world. He has exhibited at all the Association of Illustrators Annual Exhibitions and the European Illustration Annual Exhibitions since 1974 and has exhibited in London. In 1983 he set up the Central Illustration Agency, which now represents 40 of Britain's top illustrators.

1 *GERMAN MAGAZINE:*
MÄNNER VOGUE

DATE: 1988

2 *BOOK:* QUIT SMOKING
by Dr Miriam Stoppard

DATE: 1981

3 *PERSONAL CHRISTMAS CARD*

DATE: 1988

1

2

3

4

5

6

MILTON GLASER (b. 1929)

Born in New York. Attended the High School of Music and Art, then took evening classes at the Art Students League. At the Cooper Union Art School he won a scholarship in 1952 to study etching in Bologna, Italy, with Giorgio Morandi. With Seymour Chwast, Ed Sorel and Reynold Ruffins, he co-founded the Push Pin Studios in 1953 and Push Pin Graphic *in 1957, and in 1968 he founded* New York Magazine. *He was also responsible for the re-design of* Paris Match, Cue, Village Voice, New West, L'Express, L'Europeo, Jardin de Modes *and* Esquire *magazines. Books illustrated include* The Milton Glaser Poster Book *(1977),* Asimov's The Illustrated Don Juan (1972), If Apples Had Teeth *(1960) with Shirley Glaser and* Rimes de la Mère Oie *(1971) with Seymour Chwast and Barry Zaid. In 1974 he designed a huge mural for the New Federal Office Building, New York, and in 1975 designed the observation deck of the twin towers of the World Trade Center, also in New York. Glaser's distinctive work, influenced by Islamic and Indian painting and Japanese woodcuts, has won him many awards, including a gold medal from the Society of Illustrators, and in 1979 he was elected to the Art Directors Club Hall of Fame.*

1 *POSTER*

DATE: 1986

2 *BOOK:*
THE COLLECTED WORKS OF
APOLLINAIRE

DATE: 1983

3 *RECORD ALBUM COVER:*
ALBERT KING

DATE: 1976

4, 5 *END PAPER ILLUSTRATION
FOR BOOK ON GOGOL*

DATE: 1987

6 *PAINTING:*
"SHIRLEY, ANNIE AND MR
HOFFMAN"

DATE: 1985

WALTER GURBO (b. 1947)

Born in New York. After graduating from the Art Students League and the Pratt Institute, he taught at a New York public school, painting in his spare time. Recognizing that his paintings lent themselves well to magazine illustration, a friend took a selection of them to Esquire, *and this led to his first commission. Since then his illustrations have appeared in most of the major American publications, including* Village Voice, The New York Times, Esquire *and* Playboy. *Citing the diverse influences of Robert Crumb, William Blake, Max Beckmann and René Magritte, he describes his work as a combination of surrealism and expressionism. Essentially a painter, he has exhibited in New York and Florida and has recently been working on "constructions" made with acrylic paints and cardboard.*

1 *MAGAZINE:* VILLAGE VOICE
DATE: 1987

2 *MAGAZINE:* VILLAGE VOICE
DATE: 1989

3 *MAGAZINE:* VILLAGE VOICE
DATE: 1989

1

2

3

1

2

3

4

MICK HAGGERTY (b. 1948)

Born in London. Studied at the Central School of Art and Crafts, where he was influenced by his tutor, Bob Gill. After graduating in 1973 he moved to Los Angeles and set himself up as a freelance illustrator. He has worked prolifically ever since and his brightly coloured, intensely graphic illustrations have appeared in all the major American publications, including Time, The New Yorker, Playboy, Esquire, Vanity Fair *and* Rolling Stone. *He cites the soul singer Otis Redding as a major influence on his work and has taught at the Art Center in Los Angeles and the Parsons School of Design.*

I *MAGAZINE:* CHIC

DATE: 1976

2 *MAGAZINE:*
NEW YORK MAGAZINE

DATE: 1978

3 *MAGAZINE:* LA STYLE

DATE: 1987

4 "MICKEY MONDRIAN"
(uncommissioned)

DATE: 1976

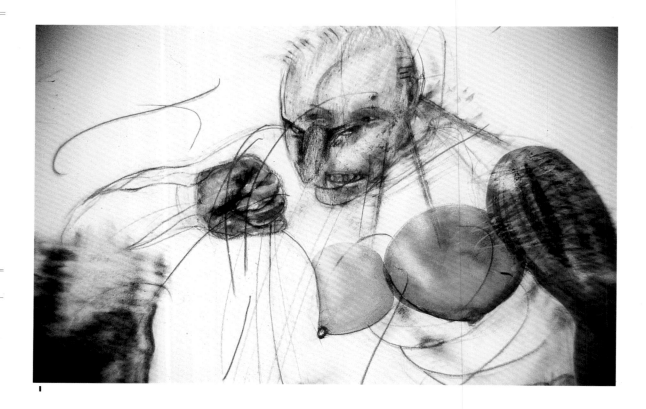

MARZENA KAWALEROWICZ
(b. 1952)

*Born in Cracow, Poland. Educated at the
Academies of Fine Arts in Cracow and
Warsaw, graduating in 1976. Since then she
has held a number of one-woman shows in
Poland, Paris, Italy, the USA and Japan.
Magazine clients include* Playboy, Gallery,
Graphis *and* Penthouse Letters *(USA),*
Gunnars *and* Mode Avantgarde *(France),*
City Life *(West Germany),* Asahigraph *and*
Illustration *(Japan) and* Projekt, Szutka,
ITD *and* Fantastyka *(Poland).*

1 *MAGAZINE:* FANTASTYKA

DATE: 1988

2 *MAGAZINE:* CITY LIFE

DATE: 1988

SUSI KILGORE (b. 1944)

Born in Marshalltown, Iowa, USA. Trained at Ringling School of Art, Sarasota, then went on to work as a staff artist for public television, as an assistant advertising director, a graphic designer and an editorial illustrator. Since 1978 she has concentrated on freelance illustration and her elegantly balanced compositions, subtle colours and great sense of action and movement have made her particularly popular with sports and news publications such as Golf, Sports Illustrated, World Report *and* US News. *Her work has also appeared in books, including* The Long March *by Harrison Salisbury (1984), on record covers, posters and TV. She has won numerous awards, including the New York Society of Illustrators Award of Merit in 1984, the Award of Excellence,* Communication Arts, *New York, in 1985 and the 66th Art Directors Annual DESI Award. She is currently illustrating* Vilma Martinez, *a learning book for Spanish students.*

1 *MAGAZINE:*
SPORTS ILLUSTRATED

DATE: 1987

2 "SWAN"
(*unpublished*)

DATE: c. 1987

3 "SHADE OF THE BEACH"
(*unpublished*)

DATE: 1988

I

2

3

LIONEL KOECHLIN (b. 1948)

Born in Paris. Trained at the Ecole Nationale Superieure des Métiers d'Art in the studio of general decoration, specializing in mural art, poster and theatre design for children. From the mid-70s he has had work published in numerous magazines, including Marie Claire, Rock and Folk, La Recherche *and* Femme Pratique. *He has also illustrated a number of books, including his own* Le Rouge, Le Jaune *and* Le Bleu *(all 1984) and Jan Van Aal's depiction of the advertising industry in France,* Au Clair de la Pub *(1986). Advertising clients include KP, Hewlett Packard, Ward Air and Mobil Oil. His influences, which include the writings of Georges Simenon and the music of Louis Armstrong, are broad and constantly changing, as is the style and content of his work. He had has exhibitions in both Belgium and France.*

1 *BOOK:*
ADVENTURES OF JOSEPH AND MIMI
by Anne-Marie Chapouton

DATE: 1988

2 *LIMITED EDITION PRINT*

DATE: 1987

3 *MAGAZINE COVER:*
THE NEW YORKER
(unpublished)

DATE: 1982

4 *UNPUBLISHED*

DATE: 1979

5 *PUBLICITY POSTER*

DATE: 1987

1

2

3

RAFAL OLBINSKI (b. 1945)

*Born in Poland. He graduated from the
architectural department of Warsaw
Polytechnical School with a distinction in
1969, since when he has achieved
international acclaim, his illustrations
appearing in* Graphis *(Switzerland),*
Novum *(Germany) and* Idea *(Japan)
magazines, and in the American publications*
Time, Newsweek, The New York Times
and Business Week. *He has also illustrated
for a number of advertising clients. He cites his
influences as "everybody", from Saul Steinberg
to Milton Glaser, Marshall Arisman and
Brad Holland, and characterizes his work as
"poetic surrealism". He has won innumerable
awards for excellence in illustration and
design, including two silver and one gold
medal from the Society of Illustrators, and is
represented at the Museum of Modern Art
(Poster Collection), at the Carnegie
Foundation in New York, and at the Poster
Museum in Warsaw, Poland. He lives in New
York, where, as well as being a freelance
illustrator, designer and painter, he teaches at
the School of Visual Arts.*

1 *PUBLICITY POSTER:*
CARNEGIE HALL CONCERT

DATE: 1988

2 *POSTER:*
"DOVE OF PEACE"
HIROSHIMA ANNIVERSARY

DATE: 1985

3 *BOOK JACKET:*
THE FOOL AND HIS MONEY

DATE: 1988

1

ROBERT PARKER (b. 1927)

*Born in Norfolk, Virginia, USA. Studied at
the Art Institute of Chicago and the
Skowhegan School of Painting and Sculpture
in Maine, where he was a pupil of Jack Levine
and Henry Varnum Poor. His intention was to
be a fine artist and he exhibited in 1952 at
Atelier 17 in New York. Successful one-man
shows followed and his work has been
acquired by the Museum of Modern Art, the
Metropolitan Museum of Art and the
Whitney Museum. His career as an illustrator
began when a series of watercolours, painted
for his son, was published in* Esquire
*magazine. This inspired commissions from
several other magazines, including the*
Lamp, Playboy, Sports Illustrated *and*
Fortune, *which sent him on several major
reportage assignments around the world. He
also worked in the film industry, producing the
canvases for Kirk Douglas's portrayal of van
Gogh in* Lust for Life, *and his watercolours
have been used on film to illustrate the poetry
of Wilfred Owen and Keith Douglas. He has
taught at the Pratt Institute, Parsons School of
Design and the Rhode Island School of Design.*

2

1 "A DOUBLE PORTRAIT"

DATE: 1986

2 "A SCENE FROM GUNGA DIN"

DATE: 1987

3 "YOU STEPPED OUT OF A
DREAM"

DATE: 1987

3

1

2

3

4

IAN POLLOCK (b. 1950)

Born in Cheshire, UK, and educated at Manchester Polytechnic and the Royal College of Art. As well as a number of one-man shows, he has exhibited in every European Illustration *Annual Exhibition and Association of Illustrators Annual Exhibition since 1975, and is represented in public collections throughout the UK, including the Victoria and Albert Museum and the Arts Council of Great Britain in London. He has illustrated for magazines such as* Rolling Stone *and* Men Only, *and recently designed the* Lear *poster for the National Theatre in London. He also does a large amount of design and advertising work, for clients such as Coopers and Lybrand, BP and Saatchis. Books illustrated include* The Miracles of Christ *(1976),* Couples *(1979)* The Pepper Press Book of Catastrophes *(1981) and* Cartoon King Lear *(1984).*

1 *POSTER*	
DATE: 1984	
2 *MAGAZINE:* MEN ONLY	
DATE: 1985	
3 "DRUNK ON THE BOWERY"	
DATE: 1987	
4 *MAGAZINE:* ROLLING STONE	
DATE: 1985	

287

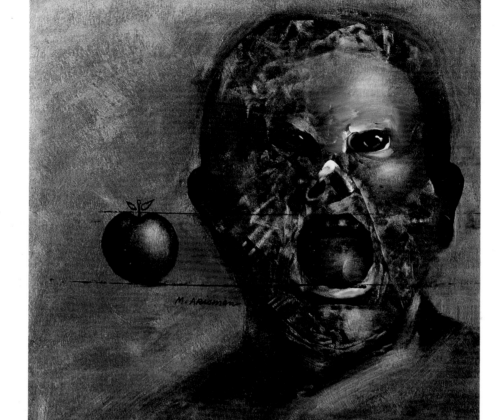

1

MARSHALL ARISMAN (b. 1938)

*Born in Jamestown, New York. On
graduating in advertising art from the Pratt
Institute in New York in 1960, he received the
Ida Gaskill Grant to travel and study in
Europe. After military service he worked as a
graphic designer for General Motors, taking
figure-drawing classes in the evenings, then
became an illustrator. He has had one-man
shows in America, Europe and Japan and his
paintings are in the permanent collections of
the Brooklyn Museum and the National
Museum of American Art. He has won
awards from the Society of Illustrators, the
American Institute of Graphic Arts, the
Society of Publication Designers and*
American Illustration. *Clients include* The
New York Times, The Nation, Mother
Jones, Time *and* Penthouse *magazines.
Books illustrated include* Fitcher's Bird
(1983) and Frozen Images, *a book of
illustrations on the theme of violence. His
influences include André François, Velázquez,
Goya, primitive art and the British painter
Francis Bacon, whose influence is particularly
evident in violent and expressive images
reflecting his concerns for the human
condition. He is currently working on* The
Last Tribe, *a series of paintings, sculpture and
video on the theme of the atomic bomb and the
future of mankind.*

1 *MAGAZINE:*
THE NEW YORK TIMES

DATE: 1986

2 *MAGAZINE:* TIME

DATE: 1987

3 *ILLUSTRATION: (unpublished)*

DATE: 1987

4 *ILLUSTRATION: (unpublished)*

DATE: 1987

5 *MAGAZINE:* OMNI

DATE: 1986

6 *MAGAZINE:* OMNI

DATE: 1985

2

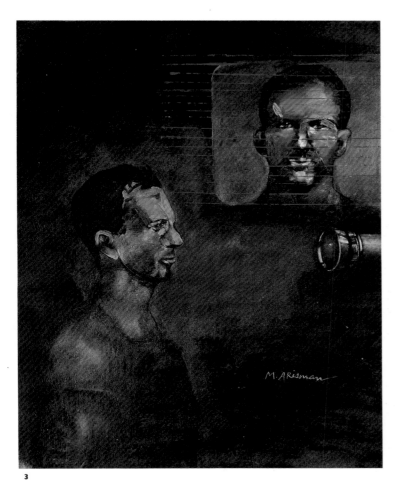

3

4

5

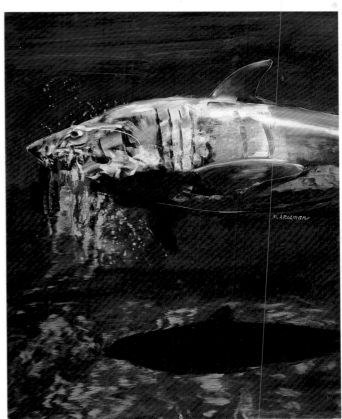

6

1

PAUL SAMPLE (b. 1947)

Born in Leeds, UK. Studied at Bradford Art College and the Central School of Art in London. Since graduating in 1968 he has become well known for his humorous illustrations, particularly those for the Smirnoff Vodka and Listerine mouthwash advertising campaigns, and cites among his influences Dudley D Watkin, H M Bateman, Heath Robinson and George Morrow. He has illustrated for newspapers including the Daily Mirror, The Sunday Times *and* Observer, *and magazines, including* Penthouse, Management Today, Men Only, Bella *and* Campaign. *Additionally he has designed book jackets for the novels of Compton McKenzie, Tom Sharpe and Flann O'Brien, and does a monthly strip cartoon,* "Ogri", *for* Bike *magazine. He works mainly in pen and ink and watercolour wash.*

I *ADVERTISEMENT:*
SMIRNOFF VODKA

DATE: 1984

2 *MAGAZINE:*
ARCHITECT'S JOURNAL

DATE: 1987

3 *BOOK JACKET:*
THE THIRD POLICEMAN
by Flann O'Brien

DATE: 1987

4 *BOOK JACKET:*
VINTAGE STUFF
by Tom Sharpe

DATE: 1983

3

2

4

1

2

3

JOHN RUSH (b. 1948)

Born in Indianapolis, Indiana, USA. Worked as an industrial designer and city planner for several years before studying illustration at Art Center College, since when he has worked as an illustrator and painter. He has lived and worked in New York, Los Angeles and Chicago and carried out assignments for a number of book and magazine publishers and advertising clients. He has won a gold medal from The Society of Illustrators and awards from the Society of Publication Designers and the Chicago Artists' Guild.

1 *ILLUSTRATION FOR:*
AMERICAN SOCIETY OF WOMEN ACCOUNTANTS

DATE: 1989

2 *ILLUSTRATION FOR:*
HUGHES UNITED PETROLEUM

DATE: 1988

3 "STUDY OF AN ARM"
(*unpublished*)

DATE: 1987

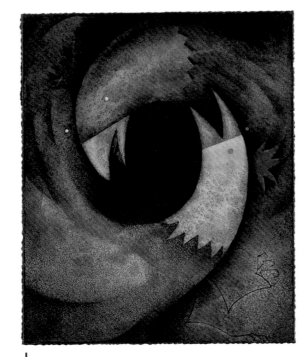

1

2

LANE SMITH (b. 1959)

Born in California, US. He graduated from the Art Center College of Design in Pasadena, California, in 1983 and moved to New York the following year to take up freelance illustration . His work is regularly included in American Illustration *and he has won a silver medal from the Society of Illustrators. In 1987 his* Hallowe'en ABC *(written by Eve Merriam) was picked as one of the ten best books of the year by* The New York Times *and the best book of the year by the* School Library Journal. *He has also published a wordless picture book called* Flying Jake *(Macmillan, 1988). Magazine clients include* New York *and* Rolling Stone.

1 *MAGAZINE:* QUALITY REVIEW

DATE: 1987

2 *BOOK:* HALLOWE'EN ABC
by Eve Merriam

DATE: 1987

3 *MAGAZINE:*
CAR STEREO REVIEW

DATE: 1987

3

ELWOOD SMITH (b. 1941)

Born in Alpena, Michigan, USA. Trained at the Chicago Academy of Fine Arts (where he studied cartoon drawing) and at the Institute of Design in Chicago. He started his career in publishing, then worked as an art director in advertising before turning to illustration. In 1976 he moved to New York, where his comic-book style of illustration featuring warm, whimsical and colourful characters was much in demand by greetings card companies, advertising clients and magazines such as Push Pin Graphic *and* New York. *An admirer of his contemporaries Seymour Chwast and Milton Glaser, as well as the cartoonists of old-time America — Rube Goldberg and George Herriman — he sees his style as a synthesis of old and new. He has won numerous awards for illustration and has written and illustrated two children's books,* The See & Hear & Smell & Taste & Touch Book *(1973) and* A Ball of Yarns *(1977). He lives in Rhinebeck, New York, and illustrates for advertising clients and magazines.*

I *NEWSPAPER:*
DALLAS TIMES HERALD

DATE: 1986

2 *MAGAZINE:*
MEDICAL SELFCARE

DATE: 1988

3 *MAGAZINE:* TIME

DATE: 1987

EDWARD SOREL (b. 1929)

Born in New York. Studied at the High School of Music and Art and Cooper Union School of Art, where he met Seymour Chwast and Milton Glaser (with whom he formed the Push Pin Studios in 1953). In 1957 he left Push Pin to concentrate on a career as a freelance illustrator and, drawn more and more to political satire, published his first cartoon book, How to be President, *in 1960. Other books include* Making the World Safe for Democracy *(1972) and* Moon Missing *(1962). His regular contributions to* Village Voice *between 1974 and 1977 were eventually published as* Superpen *(1978). He has worked for a number of publications, including* New York Magazine, Harper's, Esquire *and* The New York Times. *In 1981 he won the George Polk Award for his satirical drawings.*

1 *POSTER FOR:*
THE GRADUATE SCHOOL OF MANAGEMENT AND URBAN PROFESSIONS

DATE: 1986

2 *MAGAZINE:* GQ

DATE: 1988

3 *MAGAZINE:*
ATLANTIC MONTHLY

DATE: 1986

4 *BOOK JACKET:*
THINKING TUNA FISH, TALKING DEATH: ESSAYS ON THE PORNOGRAPHY OF POWER
by Robert Scheer

DATE: 1988

5 *MAGAZINE:*
AMERICAN HERITAGE

DATE: 1982

3

4

5

BUSH HOLLYHEAD (b. 1949)

*Born in Northumberland, UK. Trained at
Newcastle upon Tyne College of Art and
Hornsey College of Art, London. He joined
Nicholas Thirkell Associates (a subdivision of
Macmillan Publishing Ltd) in 1970 before
forming NTA Studios with three partners in
1973. He has illustrated for publishing,
editorial, advertising and design groups in 13
countries, Publishing clients include* Radio
Times, Time Out, The Sunday Times,
Design *and* Observer *magazines.
Advertising clients include Schweppes,
Cadbury's, Knorr, the Greater London
Council and the Milk Marketing Board. He
has exhibited regularly in London, Paris, New
York, Minneapolis and Amsterdam and won a
number of awards, including a Design and
Art Direction Annual silver in the UK and a
Grammy Award nomination in the US. He
enjoys composing images in which the elements
are cohesive and yet retain a sense of rhythm
and movement.*

1 *BOOK:*
THE CREATIVE HANDBOOK DIARY

DATE: 1981

2 *CALENDAR DESIGN*

DATE: 1982

3 *MAGAZINE:* THE LISTENER

DATE: 1984

BILL SANDERSON (b. 1948)

Born in Horden, Co. Durham, UK. Studied illustration at Bristol and then taught art part-time at a south London comprehensive school. In 1973, after he decided to abandon teaching and become a freelance illustrator, he presented a commissioned drawing to New Society magazine, only to be told that their letterpress printer couldn't reproduce his delicate half-tones. It was this disappointment that led him to experiment with scraperboard, a technique that he uses exclusively today. He has worked for many of the major publications in London, including The Times, Time Out, Radio Times, New Society and the New Scientist, and in America contributes regularly to Esquire, illustrating such diverse subjects as outdoor pursuits, personality profiles, the gossip columns and the sports clinic. He has advertising clients both in the UK and USA and illustrated Harry Harrison's West of Eden trilogy in 1988. As might be expected of an artist working on scraperboard, his influences are predominantly 19th century and he cites Cruickshank and Doré as particular inspirations.

1 *MAGAZINE:* NEW SCIENTIST

DATE: 1987

2 *MAGAZINE:* NEW SCIENTIST

DATE: 1988

3 *MAGAZINE:* NEW SCIENTIST

DATE: 1986

4 *CATALOGUE:* WINE SOCIETY

DATE: 1987

5 *MAGAZINE:* ESQUIRE

DATE: 1988

1

2

3

Stumble trip!
Stumble trip!
Stumble trip!

4

HELEN OXENBURY (b. 1938)

Born in Ipswich, UK. Studied at Ipswich School of Art and the Central School of Art in London, specializing in theatre design. After graduating she worked in theatre, film and television. She began illustrating children's books when expecting her first child. In 1967 The Number of Things *was published and immediately established her as a major picturebook artist. In 1970 she won the Kate Greenaway Medal for her illustrations for Lear's* Quangle Wangle's Hat *and* The Dragon of an Ordinary Family. *Since then her simple and observant watercolours have illustrated many internationally acclaimed children's books, including the* First Picture Books *(1983) and the recent* Pippo *series.*

1 *BOOK:*
DANCING CLASS
by Helen Oxenbury

DATE: 1983

2 *BOOK:* THE CHECK-UP
by Helen Oxenbury

DATE: 1983

3 *BOOK:* TICKLE TICKLE
by Helen Oxenbury

DATE: 1987

4 *BOOK:*
WE'RE GOING ON A BEAR HUNT
by Helen Oxenbury & Michael Rosen

DATE: 1989

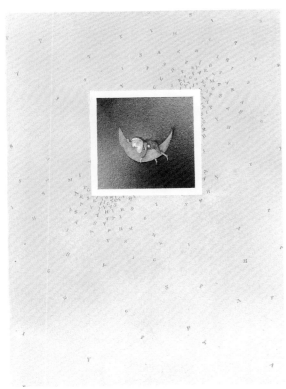

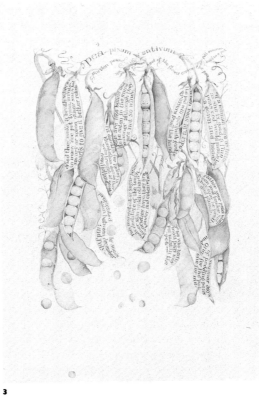

SARA MIDDA (b. 1951)

Born in Brighton, UK. Trained at Goldsmith's and Saint Martin's. Midda is much admired for her very fine, delicate and beautifully coloured illustrations, and the wonderful sense of humour which is evident in all her work. Her first book, In and Out of the Garden *(1982), in which the hand lettering is an integral part of the image, won her the Francis Williams V&A National Book League Award for Best Descriptive Illustration in 1982. She has also illustrated for* Harpers & Queen, The Sunday Times *and* Cosmopolitan *magazines and* The Guardian *and* The New York Times *newspapers. She also designs a line of products (from food packaging and babywear to bedlinen and china) under her own name for the Mitsukoshi department store in Japan. She has exhibited at the Cartoon, Langton, Thumb and Chris Beetles Galleries in London.*

1, 3 *BOOK:*
IN AND OUT OF THE GARDEN
by Sara Midda

DATE: 1982

2 *CHRISTMAS CARD*

DATE: 1984

DAN FERN (b. 1945)

Born in Eastbourne, UK. Studied graphics at Manchester College of Art and illustration at the Royal College of Art in London. As well as various advertising agencies he has illustrated for The Sunday Times, Radio Times, New Scientist *and* Design *magazines, Penguin, Pan and Time-Life books, Arista, Chrysalis and A&M records, Conran Design, Pentagram, Thames Television, the Royal Court Theatre, the BBC and the Joint Stock Theatre Group. He was a member of the jury of the Francis Williams Award for Book Illustration in 1982 and has himself won both gold and silver D&AD awards. He is a regular juror on the D&AD Annual, for whom he also runs workshops. He became Head of Illustration at the Royal College of Art in 1986, and was appointed the first Professor of Illustration at the Royal College in 1989. Fern is a designer as well as an illustrator, and his interest in stamps and printed ephemera is reflected in the letter and number forms which are often incorporated into his work. He works mainly with paper and collage, and also has an interest in computer-generated design and illustration.*

1 *WINNER'S CERTIFICATE:*
BBC DESIGN AWARDS

DATE: 1987

2 *POSTER:*
LONDON REGIONAL TRANSPORT

DATE: 1988

3 *COVER:*
ART DIRECTORS CLUB OF
HOLLAND ANNUAL

DATE: 1986

1

2

3

PETER TILL (b. 1945)

Born in Manchester, UK. He studied English Literature at Cambridge University and after graduating in 1967 worked mainly in theatre, doing illustrations as a sideline. In the early 70s he became a full-time illustrator, since when he has won a number of design and illustration awards. He has worked in advertising in Britain, Germany, Holland, the US, Sweden, Denmark and Singapore. Magazine clients include The Sunday Times, Observer, New York, Esquire, Gentlemen's Quarterly *and* Vogue. *In 1978 he made an animated film,* The Beard. *Citing Saul Steinberg as among his influences, he is entirely self-taught as an artist. His images have an element of the surreal, and he enjoys juxtaposing disparate elements as a way of inviting viewers to make their own interpretations of the work.*

1 *POSTER:* ABERYSTWYTH ARTS CENTRE

DATE: 1988

2 *MAGAZINE COVER:* THE LISTENER

DATE: 1987

3 *MAGAZINE COVER:* NEW SCIENTIST

DATE: 1987

JIM BURNS (b. 1948)

*Born in Cardiff, Wales. In 1966 he joined the
Royal Air Force as a trainee pilot, but left in
1968 to study at Newport School of Art, then
at Saint Martin's School of Art in London,
from where he received a diploma in art and
design. He has painted numerous book and
paperback covers, for Sphere, Corgi, Tandem,
Quartet, Coronet, Methuen and Fontana
Books. In 1980 he assisted Ridley Scott on
designs for the film* Blade Runner. *He has
also illustrated a series of novels by Robert
Silverberg for Bantam Books and a
collection of short stories entitled* Eye *(1985)
by Frank Herbert. Burns specializes in
historical romances and science fiction, in
gouache acrylic, watercolour and oil. A
collection of his work, featuring one hundred
colour illustrations, was published by Dragon's
World in 1986.*

1 *BOOK:* OTHER EDENS

DATE: 1987

2 *BOOK:* THE CONGLOMEROID
COCKTAIL PARTY
by Robert Silverberg

DATE: 1985

3 *BOOK:* THE CHANTRY GUILD
by Gordon R Dickson

DATE: 1988

4 "FRONTIER CROSSINGS"

DATE: 1987

5 *BOOK:* FREEWAY FIGHTER
by Ian Livingstone

DATE: 1984

1

2

3

4

5

1

2

3

4

5

6

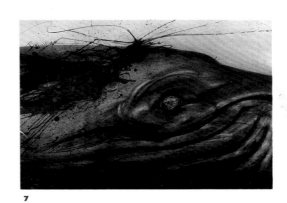

7

8

RALPH STEADMAN (b. 1936)

Born in Cheshire, UK. Studied part-time at the London College of Printing and took the Percy V Bradshaw press arts school course. He drew political cartoons for Private Eye *when it first appeared in 1961 and, at about the same time, discovered George Grosz and John Heartfield, whose powerful and caustic statements against the Establishment were a stimulus to his own work. The author Hunter S Thompson was another major influence. Their collaboration culminated in Steadman being voted Illustrator of the Year by the American Institute of Graphic Arts in 1979. His extraordinary range has ensured him equal acclaim for his children's illustrations, and his version of* Alice in Wonderland *(1967) won the Francis Williams Book Illustration Award in 1973.*

1 *BOOK:*
FEAR AND LOATHING IN LAS VEGAS
by Hunter S Thompson

DATE: 1971

2 *BOOK:*
SCAR STRANGLED BANGER
by Ralph Steadman

DATE: 1987

3 *FRONTISPIECE:*
SCAR STRANGLED BANGER
by Ralph Steadman

DATE: 1987

4 *MAGAZINE:*
SATURDAY NIGHT

DATE: 1978

5 *COLLAGE/MIXED MEDIA:*
"FALKLANDS WAR"

DATE: 1982

6 *MAGAZINE:*
ROLLING STONE

DATE: 1980

7 *MAGAZINE:* PENTHOUSE

DATE: 1979

8 *BOOK:*
ALICE IN WONDERLAND
by Lewis Carroll

DATE: 1967

RAYMOND BRIGGS (b. 1934)

Born in London. Studied at Wimbledon School of Art and the Slade School. He has written and illustrated several children's books and in 1964 his Fee Fi Fo Fum *was runner-up for the Kate Greenaway Medal, an award he won in 1966 with the publication of* The Mother Goose Treasury, *and again in 1973 with* Father Christmas. *He works in a variety of media — pencil, crayons, gouache, watercolour and line — to produce richly colourful drawings which are often presented in the format of a strip cartoon. Two of his books have been made into films:* The Snowman *(1978), the wistful story of a child's dream told entirely in pictures, was adapted by Briggs for television in 1982 and* When the Wind Blows *(1982), a despairing adult story of life after the nuclear holocaust, was made into a full-length animated feature.*

1 *BOOK:* THE SNOWMAN
by Raymond Briggs

DATE: 1978

2 *BOOK:* FATHER CHRISTMAS
by Raymond Briggs

DATE: 1973

2

1

2

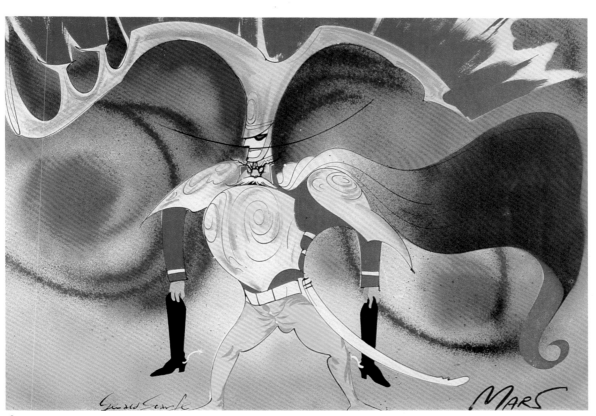

3

GERALD SCARFE (b. 1936)

Born in London. After leaving school he worked for his uncle, a commercial artist, took evening classes in figure drawing at Saint Martin's School of Art and attended drawing classes at the Victoria & Albert Museum. In 1960 he started drawing for Punch, *the* Evening Standard *and the* Daily Sketch *and in 1964 was sent by* The Sunday Times magazine *to cover the Goldwater-Johnson elections in the USA. He worked there intermittently for two years, producing several covers for* Time *magazine and working as a reportage artist. In 1966 he undertook similar projects for the* Daily Mail *and* The Sunday Times *in London. His cartoons use an exquisite sense of line to cruelly caricature political and public figures, but his satirical eye has not confined its vision to the printed page. He has had an exhibition of his papier-mâché models at the National Portrait Gallery, has designed for the theatre and opera and made animated films for the BBC and Alan Parker's feature* Pink Floyd: The Wall. *In recent years he has directed award-winning documentaries for television and is currently filming comedies for Channel 4.*

1, 2 *PUBLICITY POSTER:*
PINK FLOYD: THE WALL

DATE: 1980

3 *COSTUME DESIGN:*
ORPHEUS IN THE UNDERWORLD

DATE: 1983

307

1

PIERRE LE TAN (b. 1950)

Born in Paris. Studied briefly at L'Ecole des Arts Decoratifs in Paris before pursuing a career as a freelance illustrator. By the age of 18 he had already sold two covers to The New Yorker *magazine, and over the next few years his work appeared predominantly in such American publications as* The New York Times, Harper's Bazaar *and* Atlantic. *He illustrated the books of American author John Train and in 1977 started to write and illustrate children's stories, including* The Afternoon Cat *(1977) and* A Trip to the North Pole *(1988). The striking simplicity of his style has proved popular with advertising agencies and he has illustrated campaigns for Glenfiddich whisky in America, Manpower Services in the UK and Gallery Lafayette in Paris. Although he professes no great love of travelling, he has a column in Condé Nast's* The Traveller, *in which he visits and illustrates various locations around the world. He still lives and works in Paris, where he is taking fewer commissions and concentrating on his own adult writing. He wrote and illustrated* Rencontres d'une Vie *in 1986 and* Paris de ma Jeunesse *in 1988.*

1 *MAGAZINE:*
THE NEW YORKER

DATE: 1987

2 *MAGAZINE:* THE NEW YORKER

DATE: 1980

3 *BOOK:*
RENCONTRES D'UNE VIE
by Pierre Le Tan

DATE: 1986

4 *EXHIBITION INVITATION*

DATE: 1980

3

4

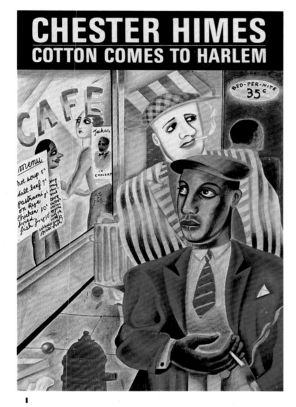

1

2

3

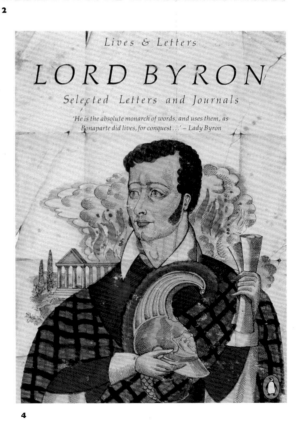

4

LAWRENCE MYNOTT (b. 1954)

*Born in London. While still at school he won a
National Portrait Gallery competition, and his
entry was a London Underground poster
publicizing the gallery. He studied at Chelsea
School of Art under Susan Einzig, whom he
cites as a major influence and who introduced
him to the illustrators of the 40s and 50s, "the
golden age of illustration". While still a
student he received his first major commission,
designing greetings cards for Jan Pienkowski's
company Gallery Five in 1973. While
studying at the Royal College of Art he
illustrated for a number of publishers and
magazines, including* Tatler *and* Vogue
*(where he has been a contributing editor on
the permanent staff since 1989). He has
taught at Hornsey, Wolverhampton and
Berkshire Art Colleges, and wrote a regular
column, "Modern Types", for the* Observer
*newspaper throughout 1987. Describing
himself as "a commercial artist rather than an
illustrator", he has designed costumes and sets
for video and theatre, and also paints portraits
and murals. He illustrates in a range of styles,
making a speciality of affectionate pastiche.*

1 *BOOK:*
COTTON COMES TO HARLEM
by Chester Himes

DATE: 1984

2 *MAGAZINE:* THE SPECTATOR

DATE: 1982

3 *MAGAZINE:* TATLER

DATE: 1982

4 *BOOK:*
LORD BYRON:
SELECTED LETTERS AND
JOURNALS

DATE: 1984

MICHAEL FOREMAN (b. 1938)

Born in Suffolk, UK. Trained at the Royal College of Art, where he won a scholarship to the USA in 1963. He was art director on Playboy, King *and* Ambit *magazines and has made animated films in Scandinavia and for the BBC in the UK. He has written and illustrated 14 books for children, including* War and Peas *(1974),* Panda and his Voyage of Discovery *(1977),* Panda and the Odd Lion *(1979) and* War Boy *(1989), and also illustrated* The Saga of Erik the Viking *(1983) and* Nicobobinus *(1986) by Terry Jones,* Tales for the Telling *(1986) by Edna O'Brien and Rudyard Kipling's* Just So *stories (1987). His expressive and sensitive watercolour illustrations have won him several awards, including the Silver Eagle prize at the Festival International du Livre, France (1972), first prize in the Francis Williams Book Illustrations Award (1972 and 1977), the Graphics Prize at Bologna (1982) and the Kurt Maschler Award (1982).*

1, 2 *BOOK:*
THE SAGA OF ERIK THE VIKING
by Terry Jones

DATE: 1983

3 *BOOK:*
WAR BOY: A SUFFOLK CHILDHOOD
by Michael Foreman

DATE: 1989

1

2

3

1

2

3

4

5

6

PAUL HOGARTH (b. 1917)

Born in Kendal, UK. Studied at Manchester College of Art and Saint Martin's. From 1946-48 he was a staff illustrator for Shell, after which he began his life as artist-traveller. Hogarth was prolific during the 50s, illustrating Jane Eyre *(1954),* The Adventures of Sherlock Holmes *(1958),* The Gold of the Snow Goose *(1958) and* King Solomon's Mines *(1958) as well as writing and illustrating* Looking at China *(1956) and* People Like Us *(1958). During the 60s he made a name for himself on the pages of* Fortune *and* Sports Illustrated *and also collaborated with Brendan Behan on books about Ireland and New York. His illustrations for Robert Graves' Poems gained him a Francis Williams Illustration Award for best illustration in 1983. His best-known works are those based on his own extensive travels, and his classic survey,* Artist as Reporter, *received the* Yorkshire Post *Award as the best art book of 1986. He has illustrated many covers for Penguin Books, including all of Graham Greene's novels since 1962. He was Senior Tutor in the Illustration Department of the Royal College of Art from 1964-70, was made a Royal Academician in 1984 and awarded the OBE in 1989.*

1 *BOOK:*
WALKING TOURS OF OLD WASHINGTON AND ALEXANDRIA
by Paul Hogarth

DATE: 1985

2—4 *BOOK:*
GRAHAM GREENE COUNTRY
by Paul Hogarth

DATE: 1986

5 *BOOK:*
NEW PENGUIN SHAKESPEARE: TROILUS AND CRESSIDA

DATE: 1989

6 *BOOK:*
NEW PENGUIN SHAKESPEARE: VENUS AND ADONIS

DATE: 1989

SEYMOUR CHWAST (b. 1931)

Born in New York. Studied graphic design at the Cooper Union School in New York, where he met Milton Glaser, Reynold Ruffins and Ed Sorel, with whom he co-founded the celebrated Push Pin Studios in 1953. After graduating he worked for The New York Times *and* Esquire, House and Garden *and* The Boston Globe *magazines. In 1953 he privately published* A Book of Battles, *and in 1985 produced his own retrospective volume,* Seymour Chwast: The Left Handed Designer. *In 1982 he and Alan Peckolick formed Pushpin Lubalin Peckolick. Clients have included leading corporations, advertising agencies and publishing companies in the USA and abroad. He has won numerous design awards, including the St Gauden's medal from Cooper Union, and was elected to the Art Directors Club Hall of Fame. He cites Ben Shahn as a major influence on his work, and the immediacy and directness of his style has become synonymous with the "Push Pin style", which has had enormous influence internationally.*

1, 4 BOOK:
HAPPY BIRTHDAY BACH
by Seymour Chwast & Peter Schickele

DATE: 1986

2 BOOK: SAM'S BAR
edited by Steven Heller

DATE: 1987

3 *THEATRE POSTER*

DATE: 1986

5 POSTER:
FORBES MAGAZINE

DATE: 1967

4

5

1

2

3

4

5

BRAD HOLLAND (b. 1943)

Born in Fremont, Ohio, USA. At 17 he left home and moved to Chicago, where he worked for a short time as a tattoo artist, then as a "short-order" artist. In Kansas City in 1964 he formed Asylum Press to print "eccentric projects with friends". In 1967 Holland moved to New York City, and contributed to various underground magazines. In 1971 he became one of the founding artists of the Op-Ed page of The New York Times. *He also designed postage stamps for the US government, executed a mural for the United Nations Building in New York, contributed to* Playboy, Time *and* Newsweek, *and wrote a book,* Human Scandals *(1977). As well as displaying an exquisite technique with both pen and brush, Holland's illustrations invariably contain powerful images, often achieved with the incongruous yet revealing juxtaposition of symbols. His work has won gold medals from the Art Directors' Club of New York, the Society of Illustrators and the Society of Publication Designers.*

1 "DETAILS AT ELEVEN"
(unpublished)

DATE: 1987

2 *MAGAZINE : FRANKFURTER ALLGEMEINE*
"MICKEY MOUSE ON SIXTH AVENUE"

DATE: 1987

3 *MAGAZINE : FRANKFURTER ALLGEMEINE*
"THE DINOSAUR LOUNGE"

DATE: 1988

4 *MAGAZINE : FRANKFURTER ALLGEMEINE*
"BLUE POOLROOM"

DATE: 1988

5 *MAGAZINE : FRANKFURTER ALLGEMEINE*
"THREE GREYHOUNDS"

DATE: 1987

ACKNOWLEDGEMENTS

RICHARD ADAMS: **262, 263;** AMNESTY INTERNATIONAL: **250;** BERNARD D'ANDREA **254;** MARSHALL ARISMAN **288, 289;** AUTHOR'S COLLECTION: **40, 72, 73, 82, 89, 221;** GUY BILLOUT: **268;** PETER BLAKE: **214;** QUENTIN BLAKE: **246, 247;** BODLEY HEAD: **253;** GLYN BOYD HARTE: **269;** BRIDGEMAN ART LIBRARY: **24, 27, 48, 49, 51, 112;** MICK BROWNFIELD: **265;** JIM BURNS: **302, 303;** DAVE CALVER: **264;** JONATHAN CAPE: **220, 224, 245, 256, 257;** PHILIP CASTLE: **267;** JEAN-LOUP CHARMET: **44, 45, 48, 50, 128, 143, 251;** CHLOE CHEESE: **271;** CHRISTIES COLOUR LIBRARY: **141** SEYMOUR CHWAST: **312, 313;** COUNTRY LIFE: **213;** TOM CURRY: **272** DAILY EXPRESS: **212** ROGER DEAN MAGNETIC STORM: **242, 243;** ANDRE DUDZINSKI: **270;** EMI: **214;** ESTATE OF M.C. ESCHER (CORDON ART BV): **170;** E T ARCHIVE: **15, 19, 23, 26, 27, 30, 31, 32, 33, 36, 38, 41, 42, 45, 46, 48, 66, 74, 76, 81, 82, 83, 87, 90, 91, 100, 113, 117, 119, 134, 135, 146, 148, 161, 168, 192, 194, 201, 203, 224, 236;** FABER AND FABER: **224, 236;** FANTAGRAPHIC BOOKS: **223;** FELMINGHAM COLLECTION: **27, 37, 41, 65, 74, 107, 117, 144, 145, 205, 218, 222, 224, 227;** DAN FERN: **300;** FOLON: **215;** MICHAEL FOREMAN: **310;** CHRIS FOSS: **274;** BERNIE FUCHS: **275;** DAVID GENTLEMAN, PENGUIN: **247;** MILTON GLASER: **278-279;** BRIAN GRIMWOOD: **277;** ROBERT GROSSMAN: **276;** GUINNESS: **225;** WALTER GURBO: **280;** MICK HAGGERTY: **281-2;** HAMISH HAMILTON: **306;** HARRAP: **159;** WILLIAM HEINEMANN: **252;** PAUL HOGARTH: **311;** JOHN HODGSON ILLUSTRATOR'S AGENCY, LONDON; **284-5;** BRAD HOLLAND: **314-5;** ICA; **251;** PETER JACKSON COLLECTION: **96, 178, 187, 204, 237;** PETER ANDREW JONES, COPYRIGHT: SOLAR WIND LIBRARY; **249;** MARZENA KAWALEROWICZ: **282;** SUSAN KILGORE: **283;** DAVID KING COLLECTION: **165, 166, 167, 172, 173;** ROGER LAW: **233;** PAUL LEITH, SHARP PRACTICE: **258;** LIBRARY OF CONGRESS: **228;** LONDON TRANSPORT MUSEUM: **120, 126, 140, 152, 156, 161, 163, 168, 169, 220;** BRIAN LOVE: **230-1;** MASTERS OF COMIC BOOK ART, AURUM PRESS: **229;** MEPL: **16, 17, 25, 30, 31, 34, 51, 42, 47, 49, 51, 52, 64, 67, 77, 86, 89, 96, 98, 99, 101, 103, 105, 106, 109, 111, 112, 113, 116, 126, 127, 131, 137, 141, 146, 147, 152, 168;** MEPL/MRS HILARY WICKHAM: **118, 119;** METHUEN: **7, 147, 157, 158, 199;** SARA MIDDA: **299;** JACQUI MORGAN: **255;** MUSEE DE LA PUBLICITE PARIS: **54, 75;** MUSEUM FUR GESTALTUNG, ZURICH: **80, 88, 95, 114, 115, 121, 129, 154, 157, 160, 182, 188, 193, 196, 201, 211, 215;** LAURENCE MYNOTT: **309;** BILL NELSON: **262;** BARBARA NESSIM: **259;** NEWMAN COLLECTION: **122, 123, 125, 133;** NIXDORF COMPUTER: **253;** RAFAL OLBINSKI: **285;** ROBERT OPIE COLLECTION: **38, 61,** 112, 118, 133, 136, 151, 152, 171, 183, 195; OUP: **183, 186, 217;** ROBERT PARKER: **286;** MERVYN PEAKE ESTATE: **184-5;** PENGUIN: **158;** BRUCE PENNINGTON AND DRAGONS WORLD: **248;** IAN POLLOCK: **287;** POLYGON EDITIONS: **180;** PUNCH: **181, 183, 187;** RANDOM HOUSE: **216;** RETROGRAPH ARCHIVE COLLECTION: **39, 44, 60, 81, 110, 114, 130, 153, 155, 157, 189, 201;** THE ESTATE OF WILLIAM HEATH ROBINSON (LAURENCE POLL) **164;** ROUNDABOUT THEATRE NEW YORK: **251;** JOHN RUSH: **291;** PAUL SAMPLE: **290;** REPRODUCED BY KIND PERMISSION OF SHELL U.K. LTD: **108, 132, 136, 151, 153, 156, 169;** LANE SMITH: **292;** LINE ILLUSTRATIONS BY E.H. SHEPARD COPYRIGHT UNDER BERNE CONVENTION AND IN THE UNITED STATES COPYRIGHT 1933 CHARLES SCRIBNERS SONS, RENEWAL COPYRIGHT © 1961 ERNEST H SHEPARD ERNEST H SHEPARD REPRODUCED BY PERMISSION OF CURTIS BROWN, LONDON: **158;** RALPH STEADMAN, SATURDAY NIGHT MAGAZINE: **305;** RALPH STEADMAN, ROLLING STONE MAGAZINE: **305;** RALPH STEADMAN, PENTHOUSE MAGAZINE: **305;** RALPH STEADMAN, ALICE IN WONDERLAND: **305;** RALPH STEADMAN, SATURDAY NIGHT MAGAZINE: **304;** RALPH STEADMAN, STAR STRANGLED BANNER: **304;** RENEE STREET: **260;** RUFUS PUBLICATIONS: **200;** SATURDAY EVENING POST/FELMINGHAM COLLECTION: **226;** GERALD SCARFE: **307;** SHELL UK LTD: **161;** ELWOOD SMITH: **293;** COLLECTION OF SOCIETY OF ILLUSTRATORS MUSEUM OF AMERICAN ILLUSTRATION: **65, 179, 207, 209, 221, 226, 235;** EDWARD SOREL: **294-5;** SPITTING IMAGE PRODUCTIONS LTD: **266;** GEOFF STEAR COLLECTION: **124;** DAVID STREET: **261;** SUNDAY TIMES/FELMINGHAM COLLECTION: **232;** SUNDAY TIMES/DAVID KING COLLECION: **233;** PIERRE LE TAN, NEW YORKER: **308;** PIERRE LE TAN: **308;** PETER TILL: **301;** THORNTON UTZ: **208;** V AND A/PHOTO EILEEN TWEEDY: **39, 43, 75, 79, 85, 86, 87, 97, 100, 108, 120, 127, 133, 136, 138, 139, 149, 150, 158, 160, 182, 197, 198, 203, 206, 210, 220;** VOGUE: **211;** WALKER BOOKS: **298;** WARD LOCK: **71;** © FREDERICK WARNE & CO., 1903, 1987: **62;** © FREDERICK WARNE & CO., 1902, 1987: **62;** © FREDERICK WARNE & CO., 1907, 1987; © FREDERICK WARNE & CO., 1907; © FREDERICK WARNE & CO., 1904, 1987; PETER NEWARK'S WESTERN AMERICANA: **68, 77, 94, 102, 107, 127;** WOMAN/AUTHOR'S COLLECTION: **234**